D0849498

Mountain Moonshine
to
Delta Gumbo

Mountain Moonshine
to
Delta Gumbo

by

W. W. (Bill) Ferguson

Delta Press
P. O. Box 6
Stoneville, MS 38776

Illustrations by Shirley Schmidt

Cover design by Lisa Brunetti

ISBN # 1-879034-00-X

Printed in the United States of America

Published by The Delta Press
              P. O. Box 6
              Stoneville, MS 38776

I wish to dedicate this book to my mother and father. It was inspired by my wife; my two daughters, Grace Williams and Judy Barnett Sims; and my three grandsons, Charles Williams, Mark Williams, and Jason Barnett.

Contents

Page

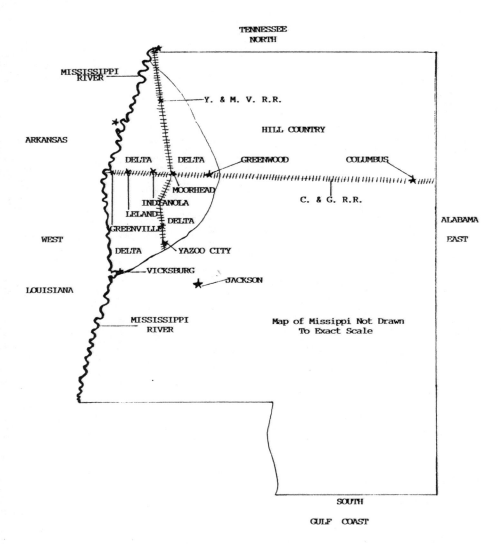

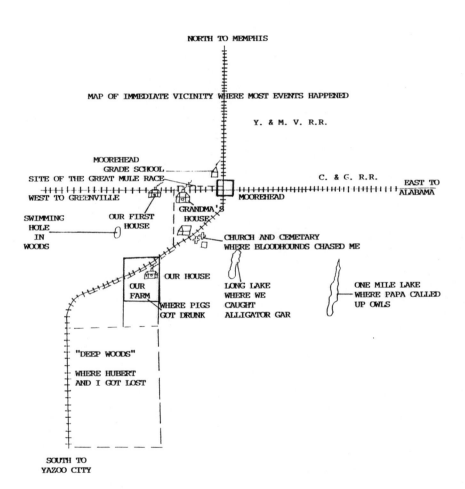

NORTH TO MEMPHIS

MAP OF IMMEDIATE VICINITY WHERE MOST EVENTS HAPPENED

Y. & M. V. R.R.

MOOREHEAD
GRADE SCHOOL
SITE OF THE GREAT MULE RACE
WEST TO GREENVILLE

C. & G. R.R.
EAST TO
ALABAMA

MOOREHEAD

SWIMMING
HOLE
IN
WOODS

OUR FIRST
HOUSE

GRANDMA'S
HOUSE

CHURCH AND CEMETARY
WHERE BLOODHOUNDS CHASED ME

OUR HOUSE
OUR
FARM

WHERE PIGS
GOT DRUNK

LONG LAKE
WHERE WE
CAUGHT
ALLIGATOR GAR

ONE MILE LAKE
WHERE PAPA CALLED
UP OWLS

"DEEP WOODS"

WHERE HUBERT
AND I GOT LOST

SOUTH TO
YAZOO CITY

Chapter 1

THE TURNING POINT

"Gilbert Ferguson, if you want to live to raise your family, it's got to be outside the state of Alabama," said the moonshiner in northern Alabama. At the time, he had pressed the cold barrel of a .44 Winchester repeating rifle into my father's ribs. "That's what we have decided," he continued, "and you know we mean business. It's your life or jail for us and we don't intend to rot in any jail."

I'll explain how my father got mixed up with the moonshiners later, but the immediate and very important move facing our family must come first.

What were we to do? There were six of us at the time, four kids and two parents. There was only one choice to make. Our Grandmother White invited us to move to her farm in Moorhead, Mississippi, which was 260 miles to the west near the Mississippi River. This move was the big turning point in our lives. We were to go by train, and none of us had been on a train before.

So, within a short time, just a few weeks, on November 27, 1917, we were standing on the wooden platform of the depot of the C. & G. Railroad in Moorhead. This was a small railroad and to make fun of it, kids called it the "Come and Go" while others called it the "Cough and Grunt," probably because of its many breakdowns.

As for me, I don't remember all of the events that took place during and just after our big trip, but I have pieced together all the important things worth telling.

One can imagine what we looked like standing there on an unusually cold day in November. My father, six feet tall, in an old wrinkled suit, made more unkempt by his sleeping in it in a box car with mules for most of two days; my mother with an old wide brimmed felt hat and a dress that dragged the ground; my older brother, Morgan, twelve years old with trousers and shirt and sweater on, bareheaded, and his hair combed straight back, the way he wore it all his life. Clara, ten, wore a dress that was almost as long as Mother's although she was just a slim, young, slip of a girl. Hubert, eight years old and I, three years and one day old, wore overalls with a shirt underneath. Only Clara had new shoes. We boys had high-topped shoes that had been half-soled by my father. But we had some things in common. We were all a little bit scared in this strange Delta town and we were all covered with soot and grime from having ridden more than 36 hours in a train car just two cars back of the locomotive.

The train's main purpose was to haul freight. Hauling passengers on that particular train was of minor importance. In those days, locomotives burned coal and the engines belched dark black smoke each time the fireman stoked the steam boiler. This smoke wafted into our passenger car through open windows for most of the trip as there was no air conditioning and one almost smothered without fresh air. The smoke had lots of charcoal in it and this had darkened our faces and our clothes. We had slept fitfully overnight on the hard, upright, leather covered seats. In addition to being sleepy and dirty, we were hungry, as we only had a basket of cold food at the start of our trip in Tuscaloosa, Alabama. At one stop my older brother, Morgan, got off the train long enough to get some sandwiches. Papa arrived in pretty good condition as he had slept with the mules in the box car.

I've thought of that trip many times. Two hundred and sixty miles in 36 hours. This was only an average of seven miles an hour. The reason for such a slow pace was that this was a freight train that stopped at almost every small town and switched cars off and on to sidings. This took lots of time. Also, numerous stops were made to take on coal and water for the engine. It was very much like the trains I saw in western movies in later years.

"Madam, [that's what Papa always called Mother], do you see that Bon Ton Cafe sign over there? Take the children over there, get the soot washed off so they won't look like darkies, and buy breakfast for them. I'll go and see to the mules back there in the box car." He had left the box car after we arrived and it had been switched to a loading dock on a siding.

The Bon Ton Cafe smelled so good, like bacon and eggs, and it was so warm and clean. It had running water and an inside toilet, something we had only seen on a few occasions but never had in our own house. What a delight it was to wash our faces in warm, clean water and sit down at a table covered with oil cloth. What I ate for breakfast I can't remember, but as my father was not there, I asked Mother about him.

"He's looking after the mules and our furniture," she said.

That one box car was only about 100 yards away and it contained all of our worldly possessions. Our simple furniture, our clothes, a few metal strap-bound trunks, and whatever keepsakes my mother had accumulated in fourteen years of marriage and in having five kids, one of which had died at birth. All of these items were in one end of the box car. In the other end were several bales of hay, a barrel of dry corn on the cob for the mules, some plows, a dismantled wagon that looked so useless with its wheels off and propped against the side walls of the car, and all other items my father owned for farming. There was even an anvil on which he hammered plow blades until they were sharp. There were no pets such as dogs or cats as we had to leave them behind. I worried about them, but Mother assured me they had been adopted by families that would care for them. I accepted her assurance as anyone three years old would.

It seemed like a week, but only two and a half days ago, we had moved all our belongings from a plain four-room house on my Grandfather Ferguson's farm, which my father cultivated and managed fifteen miles north of Tuscaloosa. My grandfather furnished two wagons, drivers and mules and we took our only wagon. All three were heavily loaded and quite often we had to get off the wagons and walk, sometimes even pushing, to help get the wagons over the rather steep hills. The roads were only of dirt but were dry as it hadn't rained for some time. This fifteen-mile ride required one full day as we had to stop and feed and rest the mules.

In Tuscaloosa, we spent the night with my father's sister in a big, modern house. Her husband was a doctor and they had all sorts of nice things I had never seen before. Hubert and I were put to bed in a feather bed. I had heard of them but had never slept in one. When I climbed into bed and lay down it seemed I would sink forever and would end up being smothered. Our own beds had cotton mattresses and they got hard after a few years' use.

Most of the next day was spent loading the box car. As it had some loose hay on the floor, it looked like a good place to sleep, but only my father was allowed to sleep in it. His excuse that he had to look after the mules was accepted by the conductor who would not let anyone else ride in the box car. So, we had to ride in the passenger car near the front of the train.

To a three-year-old, this trip was a big adventure, but it was to the others, too. It was a brand new experience and we enjoyed looking at the hills and trees until we all became sleepy. Being the smallest, of course I made use of my mother's lap. Poor Mother, I wonder if she got any sleep at all.

Soon after starting, I asked her, "Mother, why are we leaving home and going away? I'd rather stay home with Grandpa."

"Don't worry," she replied, "some day you will know we have a good reason." This didn't answer my question, but I knew it was no use to continue to question her. I just had to take things as they came or were given to me.

Mother was always quiet-like and philosophical about life and she, too, took things as they came without complaint. I suppose Mother must have been a very unusual person as she gave birth to a total of twelve children, all in her home, but there was a doctor or mid-wife there to help each time. She bore the sorrow of three of them dying either at birth or soon after stoically. But I was too young to understand the deep hurt she must have suffered over their loss.

And how could a mother have time for and love so many kids? I'll never know the answer and the question never even came to mind when I was a young boy. But she did love each of us. Years later, she wrote each of us letters, laboriously in long hand. She even wrote her grandchildren later in life. We always called her "Mother" with no exceptions and it always seemed strange for us to hear other kids refer to their mothers as "Mama." Somehow or other that word didn't do justice to our mother. Father was always "Papa," but that was not so strange as "Daddy" was not in common use in those days.

When we arrived, Moorhead had a population of about 900, of which 600 were black and 300 white. It was known as the hub of the Delta because, surprisingly, it had two railroads, which crossed there. Moorhead became known over the state as the place where the Southern (the C. & G. which we rode east and west) crossed the Yellow Dog (the Y. & M. V. Railroad which ran north and south from Memphis, Tennessee on the north to Yazoo City, Mississippi on the south).

Moorhead's streets were sandy but became muddy after heavy rains. Wagons lined the sides of the streets as there were only three cars in town. The store fronts had ten-foot metal eaves which protected those who were on the sidewalks. The Bon Ton Cafe where we ate and the three story Phoenix Hotel did a good business as many salesmen changed trains at Moorhead and were forced to buy food and stay over-night there. All transportation went by railroad or wagon. There were no buses until years later. The whole countryside was flatter than a pancake as compared to the beautiful hill country we left. No pine trees grew in the Delta. All trees were hardwood, such as oak, elm, and pecan.

When we were forced to leave Alabama by the moonshiners, a fact I didn't know at the time, the only good choice my father had was to accept Grandmother White's invitation to manage and cultivate her 160-acre farm which she bought with an inheritance a few years before.

Grandmother White went a little overboard when she built her own house. It was huge, with fourteen-foot ceilings, which made it cooler in summer, porches on two sides, and an inside bathroom. Imagine such luxury: an inside bathroom. Her well had been drilled 1500 feet deep just like the one in Moorhead and it was an artesian well which flowed without any pump for over forty years. Its water was very soft and tasted so good.

Her lighting system was the latest thing to be found outside a town that had electricity. It was by carbide gas. Carbide was mixed with water and produced a gas which ran through pipes in the house. Each room had two or more gas lights on the walls, just high enough to be out of the reach of young kids. Each gas jet had a mantle and globe over it. To light the jet one turned a valve, lighted a match and the gas coming from the jet caught fire. This caused the mantle to glow just like lights campers used at night many years later. This was almost like magic to kids such as we, who had only had kerosene lamps and lanterns to light our home and read by at night. We were used to four of us crowding around a small table and reading by the kerosene light.

People came from miles around by wagon to fill jugs and pails with the fine, soft water from Grandmother's well and quite often she invited them into the house which, as my father said, "was a curiosity to them."

The whole house was a curiosity to us, too, but we lived in a four-room home without running water or lights which Grandmother had built about 200 feet from her home. It faced the C. & G. Railroad which we had arrived upon and we always saw all the trains go by.

Grandmother White, my mother's mother, was a tall sort of raw-boned woman without an ounce of fat on her. She coiled her long hair on top of her head just as my mother did. Grandma had a good sense of humor and told funny stories to us kids. Later, I heard she told some that were not so nice when talking to adults. Grandmother White, who had lost her husband years before, had four kids: three girls, of which my mother was one, and one boy, the youngest child. This boy had gone into the Army, as the war with Germany was on in 1917, and was overseas. From what my mother and her sisters said, Grandma had spoiled her son something awful and had even bought him an expensive car, a Franklin with twelve cylinders, before he went to serve in the Army.

Grandma was kind and generous to everyone, it seems, but what was not understandable to me was that she dipped snuff. Of course, that was a common habit among women of the South in those days, but my mother never did. Grandma would send me out to cut small twigs off elm trees to make her snuff brushes from. I then peeled the bark off the twigs and hammered one end of the twig until the end was a mass of fibers. Grandma then wet the brush and dipped it into the snuff bottle. Then she placed the snuff brush coated with snuff in her mouth and rolled it around her mouth with an expression of pleasure on her face. I guess she was getting a nicotine high from the snuff. The last time I saw Grandma she was still dipping snuff.

While Uncle Robert, Grandma's son, was in the Army, one of her daughters, Inez, learned to drive the Franklin, or at least she tried to learn. A single garage with two doors was built for the Franklin which was one of the three cars to be found for miles around. Aunt Inez propped one door open but could find no prop for the other door one day when she wanted to back the car out. Although I was about four years old at the time, she asked me to stand by the door and hold it open as she backed out. I did this as she got in the car. One of the black men who worked for Grandma cranked the engine with a crank attached to the front of the car. Aunt Inez put it in reverse gear and started backing out. She didn't back straight out and the rear bumper hit the door I was holding open for her. The door was knocked off its hinges and fell on top of me. Although I wasn't seriously hurt, Aunt Inez thought at first that she had killed me. Such weeping and wailing I had never heard in my life. Everybody came running from all directions. I guess I was just a bit addled by the blow, but to make matters worse, one of the metal hinges struck the thigh of my right leg and knocked a pretty big hole in it. When I saw the blood spurting all over, of course, I, too, thought I had been badly injured. So, someone, not Aunt Inez, because she was too unstrung to drive, drove me to town where stitches were used to close the wound. The scar from that wound has stayed with me all my life. In time, Aunt Inez got over the shock and drove the Franklin all over the countryside.

It was very kind of Grandmother White to invite us to live near her and have a place to work, but only two years had passed when my father realized the farm was too small to support two families. He began to look for other places to farm and also began planning to buy his own farm if his father back in Alabama would consider either lending him some money or advancing him part of the inheritance he expected to receive at my grandfather's death.

Two events happened while we were living near Grand-mother White that are indelibly written in my memory. One had to do with a rabid dog (a "mad dog" as they were called) and the other had to do with a terrible tornado. But first, I must tell you about the moonshiner's forcing us to leave our Alabama home and move to Mississippi. We gradually overcame the shock of change which was almost like moving to a foreign country, and our family also grew to a total of six boys and three girls here.

Chapter 2

"LEAVE ALABAMA OR DIE— IT'S YOUR CHOICE"

Kids have a way of eavesdropping when they shouldn't and I was no exception. But how else can a youngster find out things about his family? Oldsters just don't think a kid needs to know certain things about the family and don't volunteer to tell them some of the most interesting and sometimes most fearsome things that have happened in the past.

It was by eavesdropping when I was about eleven years old that I got some of our family's background that made me wonder if I really knew my father as I thought I did. What I heard one night when I was supposed to be trying to read in an adjoining room fully answered the question I had asked Mother on the long train ride from Alabama. I had asked her, "Mother, why are we leaving Grandpa Ferguson's farm and our home and going so far away?"

My father, mother, and older brothers, Morgan and Hubert, were sitting around the open fireplace when Hubert dared to ask my father to give them the full story of why the family came to the Mississippi Delta country. Of course, it was Hubert who would have the nerve to ask in the first place.

My father's answer was a story in itself that started out pretty dull at first. I almost lost interest, but then it picked up in excitement and from that point on I didn't miss a word he said, although he didn't know I was listening.

"Boys, you are now old enough to know what happened back there in Alabama and I guess you have wondered many times.

"Of course you know that I managed your Grandfather Ferguson's farm in the hills north of Tuscaloosa. We had our own little four room house. You know the North River ran nearby, cutting the farm in two. The surrounding country was hilly and covered with pine trees. In places the hills were rocky and you boys climbed those hills and rolled rocks down their sides. You remember the ford on the river when the river was low in summer and we drove the wagons across it. And I suppose you saw the veins of coal that stuck out of the sides of the river banks and how we broke the coal into chunks with sledge hammers and burned it in our stoves for heat in winter.

"You can remember all those things, and you knew that we were farmers. Your Grandfather Ferguson was not only a farmer, but he also was a Baptist Minister circuit rider who traveled from country church to country church preaching every Sunday. He was away so much that it was my job to manage his large farm. He was a veteran of the Confederate Army, but that's another story.

"In those wooded hills and small mountains there were caves where an outlaw could have hidden for months if he had enough food and water. In fact, there were outlaws there, but they made moonshine whiskey and were known as moonshiners. Their whiskey stills were crude but they did the job.

'The State of Alabama had its own law against making, selling, or drinking whiskey and had its own officers to enforce the law. This was before the United States Government passed the Volstead Act in 1918 which was about like Alabama's law.

"What will surprise you is that I was an undercover agent for the State of Alabama. It was my job to locate those illegal stills and report by mail or courier to the officers in Tuscaloosa. Their problem was to catch the moonshiners with the still in operation. I was to remain in the background and never be seen."

You could have heard a pin drop because everyone was so quiet. My excitement grew just to think my father had done such a daring thing.

He continued, "I was a 'revenueer', but it had to be a complete secret except for the madam [my mother]. We suspected that some of those moonshiners sat beside us every Sunday in church and put some of their ill-gotten gains in the offering plate. These same men were busy quite often, out at night making whiskey in the caves or canebrakes of the hills."

"What was a whiskey still like, Papa?" Hubert asked.

"The easiest way to describe a still is to say it is a heavy cast iron pot which is closed at the top except for a small outlet. From this outlet runs a coiled copper pipe which is laid in a trough of cool water. This tube is several feet long and leads to a container such as a glass jar. The pot is heated and the mixture in it, 'mash', turns partly to steam and runs out under pressure. This steam is then condensed in the cooled tube back into liquid. This is the whiskey and it drains into the container. Stills were cheap to make and almost anyone could have one. Making whiskey was the livelihood for quite a few of the hill people who had a hard time just eking out a life in those surroundings.

"My boss had recruited me as an undercover agent in 1916 and my heart was really in my work as my family were teetotalers and never drank whiskey or wine. My father preached about the sins of drinking often in his Sunday sermons. I had been taught that whiskey making was not only against the law, but one of those dreadful sins.

"It wasn't difficult to hide the location of the whiskey stills but it was difficult to hide the location of the mash from which whiskey was made. Mash was made by mixing cornmeal, rye meal, sugar, water, and a small amount of yeast and letting the mixture ferment for about 48 hours. When it began to bubble the moonshiner knew it was ready to distill. In fact, he knew he must do it right away, for its alcoholic content was highest when it began to give off bubbles. As it had a very strong odor that seemed to cling to the ground, it could be smelled for at least 250 yards down wind. My job was to locate the stills and let my boss know when it would be ready to distill. The officers had to catch the moonshiners in operation in order to have an air-tight case against them. It was up to them to do the catching; I was to do the spotting.

"One day I came up from the downwind side of a very dense canebrake and just before walking up to it, smelled that unmistakable odor of mash. It's a sour odor like no other. I lay down in the grass and weeds after making my way up to the small forest of bamboo we called cane, which grew about twenty to thirty feet high, and in a mass was known as a canebrake. The only noise I heard was that of a protesting bluejay and the raucous call of a crow in the distance. After being certain there was no person nearby, I went gingerly and noiselessly around the canebrake. Sure enough, I found it—a path, small and crooked, but well trodden, leading into the middle of the canebrake which was about fifty yards wide.

"After pausing again and hearing no noise, I followed the crooked path. After about twenty-five yards, there it was. A clearing just large enough for four large wooden vats of mash and an old well-used whiskey still, alongside of which were some crude chairs and benches. Off to one side was a pile of wood used to fire the still which sat in the middle of the clearing. Across the tops of the vats of mash, gunny sacks had been draped to keep insects out. These sacks did keep the flies out, but they were covered with all kinds of insects which were trying to get to the ill smelling mash below.

"All the while I was frightened for my safety, as someone could noiselessly come up the crooked path, just as I had a few moments before. If this happened, most likely it would be one of the moonshiners coming to check on whether the mash was bubbling or not and he would be armed with a rifle as most moonshiners were. He could easily get the drop on me while I was busy examining the still. All I had for protection was a .38 caliber revolver. This would be plenty, in most cases, but not from a Winchester, which would be pointed my way before I could draw. Luckily, no one came upon me and my examination indicated the mash would be just right in its fermentation process to distill within about 48 hours.

"I got the word to my boss in Tuscaloosa by overnight mail. Being an undercover agent meant that I was never to be identified when a raid was made on a still. I was to remain in the dark shadows of the canebrake while the officers made the arrests. Otherwise, the moonshiners would know me as an agent and my days would be numbered. There would be no way I could continue to live in that area of the country.

"My boss in Tuscaloosa sent a secret message by horse courier that I must be sure the still was actually in operation before he could organize a raid on it—the moonshiners must be caught red-handed in the act of making whiskey. Most whiskey making was done at night, as the smoke from the fire under the still would hang in the valleys by day and be a dead giveaway as to the still location. So, he instructed me to go out again the second night later, to be sure the distilling operation was in progress. Oh Boy! I hated going it alone, when I knew these mountain men were almost as good as Indians detecting any strange movement or sound in the dead of night. But I had to go as it was my duty and I also believed in what I was doing. The night arrived and I prepared myself as best I could. First, I chose dark clothes and dark hat. Then I rubbed some charcoal from the end of a burned-out faggot from the fireplace on my face and hands. I also made certain my shoes didn't squeak."

By this time, the story was getting pretty long and I was getting restless, but I knew something very important was coming up soon, so I listened through the open doorway. At this point, Papa bit off a chew of fresh Brown Mule tobacco, spit on the open fire, and continued.

"I reached the general area hurriedly, but when near, I made my way softly and quietly, up the path which led to the still. I tried not to break a dead stick, snap a twig, or make the slightest noise. Through the cane, I could see lots of activity. The flames under the still caused shadows to eerily dart back and forth, causing me to suspect movement nearby when all was still. Smoke was rising straight up as if from a chimney in the calm air and a gallon jug at the end of the copper tube was about half full of the amber moonshine whiskey. Since I had been there two days before, someone had moved in a large number of fruit jars, usually used in canning fruit and vegetables by the hill farmers. Several of these were already full. Right away, I recognized three tenant farmers who lived in the vicinity on nearby farms and who occupied the same group of pews in church our family sat in on Sundays. What a surprise, but the real surprise was yet to come.

"As it does most times, bad trouble came unexpectedly. Suddenly, I felt a hard, cold object pressed firmly against my back and heard a command.

" 'Put your hands up and don't turn around.'

"I felt helpless and was scared speechless. There in the dark, except for flickering shadows caused by the distilling fire twenty yards away, I knew my life was in danger—the hard object was the muzzle of a Winchester .44 rifle and without a doubt it was loaded.

"The holder said, 'Hold still while I search you.' He patted me down and quickly removed the .38 Smith and Wesson revolver in my shoulder holster.

"After removing the pistol he said, 'Turn around.' When I complied, he exclaimed, 'Of all things, it's preacher Ferguson's son, Gilbert. What are you doing here?'

"Desperately, I tried to think of a reasonable answer. 'I was out possum hunting and hoping to find a persimmon grove with a possum up a tree,' I lamely said.

" 'That's a lie and you know it. Whoever heard of someone hunting for possums without a light and with a .38 instead of a shotgun?' He poked me in the ribs and said, 'I'll give you 30 seconds to tell the truth or you will be buried in one of these nearby caves before the night is over.'

"I knew the jig was up and I had just as well tell the true story. So I did, knowing that there was no easy way out for me in any case. After I told him I was an undercover agent for the state liquor control agency, he believed me and said, 'Just stand here in the light of the fire while we hold a meeting to decide what to do with you.'

"So the question was, what would they do with me? All of them knew me, but the only one whom I could say was a friend of our family and of my father, was the one who held the gun on me in the first place, Josh Friendly. Of course, he wasn't very friendly that night. Maybe Josh would have a little mercy, but I doubted the others cared what happened to me.

"After some heated remarks, which I couldn't understand, Josh came back and said, 'The boys say you have two choices. If you stay around here we will bushwhack you on some lonely road, either night or day, and your wife and kids will be without a father, or you can leave the State of Alabama within thirty days and live. Which do you choose?"

"My decision was quick in coming. I knew they meant business and I also knew my career as an undercover agent for the State of Alabama had come to an abrupt end.

"So I said, 'I'll move out of the State of Alabama to Mississippi where my wife's mother owns a farm. She wants me to manage it.'

" 'All right,' he said, 'but you be quick about it.'

"Suddenly, my relief was so great that I was almost overcome and thanked them profusely for sparing my life. But this wasn't the end of the matter.

"These moonshiners knew I came from a family who thought whiskey was an evil, and never drank it. The truth is, I had never tasted whiskey in my life. They knew how I felt about whiskey. In their little pow-wow they had decided to punish me even if they did spare my life.

"Josh said, 'Gilbert, here is a freshly distilled pint of whiskey, and you've got to drink it without any water or anything else, and we mean quick.'

"Never having tasted whiskey, I had no idea how terrible it tastes and what a shock it can be to one's system. With a gun in my back, I took a swallow, but gagged and could not continue— that is, I thought I couldn't.

"He shoved the gun harder into my ribs and said, 'Drink.'

"I held my breath and consumed about one-half the pint before taking the fruit jar down from my lips. My throat felt like it was on fire and my stomach, too, seemed to be burning up, but I was only half through. Since that time, I've heard a pint of pure whiskey can kill a man. Finally, I drank the last drop, but in moments I lost consciousness and knew nothing of what followed.

"My next conscious thought came the next morning when I awoke to find myself lying in a thicket of briars with the sun shining in my face. I was still in the woods and felt only half alive. There was no compass to use and no landmark I recognized but I knew home had to be southwest unless they had moved me miles away while I was unconscious.

"So I headed southwest and finally came to a road I recognized. From there I went south another mile or two, stumbling all the way and wondering if I could ever make it. When I reached home my family was in a state of panic. They had notified everyone for miles around that I was missing, but only the madam knew of my undercover work and she had taken an oath of secrecy about it. Morgan, Hubert, and Clara knew I was missing one whole night but they never knew why until now. The madam told the neighbors I must have gotten lost while hunting."

I sat quietly for awhile, pretending to be reading, but letting his story sink slowly in. Now, I thought, I have the answer to the question I asked Mother on the train from Alabama.

Another thought came to mind. Papa wasn't just an ordinary dirt farmer, living a drab and uneventful life. He had done exciting things I didn't even know about and I knew I would look at him anew as if he were something pretty special. Suddenly, it hit me. Papa had a .38 Smith and Wesson in a shoulder holster in the closet and I knew he met strange men from Clarksdale in the evenings and went to places he never talked about. Could it be that he was again an undercover agent, but this time for the U.S. Government? Something told me that he not only could be but most likely was.

Chapter 3

A DIFFERENT COUNTRY—THE DELTA

When we stood on that cold, deserted railroad depot platform in Moorhead, having just arrived, mules and all, from Alabama in November of 1917, the only pretty thing I could see was the Bon Ton Cafe. As I was only three and couldn't read, my older brother who was in the second grade told me it was a place to eat. So it looked pretty to me as I was hungry and tired after 36 hours on a slow train.

After a quick look around, I decided most of what I could see was ugly. After coming from the pretty, pine tree-covered hills of Alabama, I was in a place where all the trees looked like bare skeletons, having lost their leaves after an early frost. People had told us the land was as flat as a pancake and they were telling the truth. In fact, most of what we had heard about the Delta came from those rare persons who had traveled there with the intentions of settling down and making their homes, but instead, had grown discouraged and gone back to Alabama.

Moorhead had about 900 people. The streets were covered with gravel. The two railroads crossed each other in the center of town. There were a few stores, a bank, and a post office. All store fronts had wide, overhanging roofs of tin to protect those who walked along in front of them from the rain. Later, when older, I found that the strangest thing about Moorhead was that it had a high school with dormitories for students. People from as much as 150 miles around sent their kids to school there and they lived in these dormitories and went to school. The school had a farm, a dairy herd, and shops, almost like a community. I was to go there later, but of course, I didn't live in the dormitory as we lived only two and a half miles from the school and could walk that distance.

Most people know what a Delta is—it's land, usually very flat, that is formed by sedimentation from a muddy water. Most people also think the Mississippi River Delta is only near the mouth of the river where it enters the Gulf of Mexico, but this isn't true. There is Delta land on either side of the Mississippi River all the way from Cairo, Illinois, to the Gulf of Mexico. All of this land, except that where the forests had been cleared away for farming, was covered by hardwood trees such as oak, pecan, ash, elm, hackberry, and sweet gum. The soil is very rich and productive.

Indians had lived in our part of the Delta until about 1890. They hunted and fished and raised a very few crops such as corn and vegetables. As the land had flooded often from the Mississippi River overflowing its banks, the Indians had built huge earthen mounds, known by us as Indian mounds, as a haven in case of floods. These mounds were as much as 100 feet in diameter and twenty to thirty feet high. They were also used in some of their native ceremonies. All the soil was carried to the spot in hand baskets. It always seemed impossible that they could build such huge earthen mounds this way, but they did. Some of these mounds were used for cemeteries. I know this is true because I saw some skeletons uncovered when a highway right of way required that bulldozers cut through the side of an Indian mound. An uncle of mine had some of the bones from these unearthed skeletons in a cabinet at home. When I looked at them, I got a sort of sick feeling, but must admit that I wondered if they were the bones from some Indian brave or maiden. There was no way for us to tell which it might have been.

To make the Mississippi Delta inhabitable, the U.S. government built huge dikes, or levees as we called them, on each side of the Mississippi River where needed, from Illinois to the Gulf. Without the levees the land would have flooded almost every year, but when we settled in the Delta in 1917 they had already been constructed. Also, the Delta had hundreds of small drainage canals known as dredge ditches, dug by dredging machines, to carry off excess water during the winter rainy season. During this season most of the land became a bog and roads were impassable if not covered by gravel; even the Model-T Ford school buses couldn't run every day. On those days we rode mules to schools. We could tell whether to saddle up the mules by just looking at the road in front of our house. Delta folks called the black, sticky mud "gumbo."

Those dredge ditches not only made the land more useful for farming, but they also offered us lots of fun. There were low spots in them that held water even during the dry summer season. These low, stagnant water holes were ours to use for swimming pools. With no public pools anywhere for many miles around, we used these pools of algae-covered water for swimming. We shared these pools with frogs, snakes, small fish, and anything that lived in such water, including millions of tadpoles. Wild animals in the woods such as rabbits, raccoons, squirrels and birds came to drink at dawn and dusk.

It was four or five years after we arrived from the pretty hills of Alabama before I began to adjust to living in the Delta where about seventy-five percent of the entire land was covered by woods and seventy-five percent of the inhabitants were black people who gathered in town on Saturday night. The stories about bad things found in the Mississippi Delta were mostly true, but we got adjusted to the surrounding country and began to enjoy life, although living was pretty difficult for us. It required a little more than five years for me to understand exactly where we were in relation to other things of importance. It was thirty-five miles as the crow flies to the Mississippi River on the west, 125 miles from Memphis, Tennessee, on the north, ninety-five miles to Vicksburg on the south, and thirty miles to the Mississippi hills on the east. Moorhead, small though it was, became known as the hub of the Mississippi Delta because it was in the very middle of it. Being the hub of the Delta didn't mean that it would grow all that much because it was never larger than two thousand people. This was probably because it was not the county seat.

Still, it was our hometown. It was where we bought all our food, mostly from grocery stores owned by Chinese who had come up the Mississippi River as crewmen on river steamers. They had jumped ship somewhere, migrated inland a few miles, and after a few years as store clerks, set up their own businesses. Moorhead was where we formed our first genuine lasting friendships. Our doctors lived there. It was where my father borrowed money and paid ten percent interest to banks when he was only charging those who borrowed from him (black tenants) six percent. It was there that we went to the Baptist church where I was "born again," as were most of my brothers and sisters. It was from Moorhead that we were banned on Saturday nights by our father because of the danger of getting hurt, even as innocent bystanders. Fights with knives and guns were no novelty on that one night of the week when the day laborers came to town. They came with money in their pockets, a desire to drink too much of the bootleg whiskey available, and even a stronger desire to "treat the ladies." It was my home town and eventually I grew proud of it.

We always knew malaria was around us at all times but our family had a screened house and kept mosquitoes out most of the time. We knew some of those mosquitoes carried malaria and could give it to us if they bit us. For years, however, none of us had the chills and fever that result from having malaria in one's bloodstream. We heard of many cases where more than one in the family had malaria.

One pretty spring day I went to school feeling just fine and ready for anything I might confront that day, but at about 11 a.m. things began to change for me. I began to feel cold and to shiver, even to shake all over my entire body. At the time I was feeling so cold, the teacher found my forehead to be very hot.

She immediately took me to the first-aid room, put me on a cot, covered me with two quilts, (although it was a warm, sunny day), and took my temperature. It was up to about 102°. This was not all *that* frightening, but alarmed her so she called a doctor. He told her I was having a chill associated with malaria. He said she should give me aspirin to hold my fever down but keep me covered with blankets until I got over the chill and felt normal again.

After about two and a half hours I began to feel good again and by the time school was out that day I felt just fine, except maybe a little weak.

My folks bought a "through" of Quinine from the druggist the next day and got me started on taking the capsules every so many hours. But it was a little too late because exactly two days after the first chill, and at the same time of day, I had another chill at school. Again, I had the same treatment in the first-aid room.

The doctor said, "Don't worry, he won't have another if he takes his Quinine on schedule."

The doctor was right. I did take my Quinine on schedule for twenty-one days and had no malaria again in my life. But I surely learned lots about malaria.

The protozoan causing malaria has a forty-eight hour life cycle. When the mosquito puts it into one's blood stream, it enters the red blood cells and breaks out in the form of many protozoa. This continues each forty-eight hours until so many red blood cells are killed and so much poisonous waste is remaining in the blood stream after each cycle that the body reacts with a chill such as I had. If this is allowed to continue too long the body becomes weaker and weaker and eventually one could die. Thousands did before the cure of malaria was found, and at that time it was Quinine. Later, a drug named Atabrine was invented and used to prevent malaria in the first place, as well as cure it, but this was years after my experience.

The reason one had to take the proper amount of Quinine for twenty-one days was to be certain the Quinine was in the blood stream in such quantities as to kill the malaria germs each time they broke out of the blood cells. As all of them did not break out at the exact same time, after a person had been a victim for a month or so, it was necessary to continue the treatment until one was sure they had all been killed.

28

I had heard about those chills from other kids, but I had no idea how severe and frightening they were until I experienced them myself. Luckily, I never had malaria again. Malaria was rampant in the South when I was growing up but later it was almost totally eliminated as an illness by the use of Quinine and Atabrine.

Baby Ruth, a little sister, came into our world at home with a doctor in attendance, just like all the other eleven did. But for some reason she seemed to be the pet of the family. All of us kids seemed to treat her almost like a doll. She was no different from other babies, or at least that's what we thought. She was gurgly and smiling most of the time, but like other babies she could make her wants and discontents known by crying in a strong healthy way.

Why did she have to get pneumonia? I've always asked myself that question. I was twelve and spent quite a bit of time rocking her to sleep or giving her the bottle she seemed to always be wanting. Because of my having her in my arms so much she became very dear to me. With so many other kids around, Mother was constantly busy, so it was natural that one had to help look after Baby Ruth's wants. I never knew why we all called her Baby Ruth. It was as if Baby was one of her names, but it wasn't.

When Baby Ruth was six months old, still too young to crawl or do hardly anything for herself, she became ill and began to run a high fever. Naturally, Mother got in touch with Dr. Wasson who came out from town in his T-Model Ford to have a look at her. In those days doctors came to your home to see you if you were sick. Transportation was still a problem, but all doctors had cars and could come to the sick if the gravel roads were in passable condition.

We were all concerned when Dr. Wasson said she seemed to have pneumonia. He didn't X-ray her as there were few X-ray machines in those days, but I guess he could tell her problem by listening to his stethoscope. Anyway, he prescribed some medicine which he had in his kit and told Mother to keep cool wet cloths on her head.

"Try to keep her fever down, is the idea," he said.

But her temperature wouldn't stay down and she developed a cough; a big, deep cough for such a little baby. And I noticed how hard she was breathing. It seemed every breath was so hard for her to get. It was so noisy, her breathing, that is, that in that quiet house, it could be heard in all the rooms.

All of us were so sad and despondent because there was just nothing we could do. We tip-toed around the house. There was no playing, joking, or running through the house. It was as though we thought our being so quiet would make her well.

Dr. Wasson came many times and did all he could do. One night about six he came when her fever had reached 105°.

We were all huddled around her bed when he said, "Maude [that was my mother's name], if her fever doesn't break in the next twelve hours, I'm afraid we will lose her. Her only hope is that her body will overcome the pneumonia. If it does you will know it almost immediately, but if it doesn't, you will know that also."

So we all waited, watched and listened. Instead of getting lighter, her breath came in great gasps for such a little baby. In about two more hours, after two long gasps for breath, her little body gave up the fight. For the first time in my life I knew what death really meant. It was one of the few times I ever saw my mother cry and tears ran down my father's face. Even with so many children, each was precious, and each had a special place in our father's and mother's hearts.

I had never known anything about a funeral. I didn't even know what was done to prepare for one at that time. Of course, things changed as the years went by, but I remember Ruth's funeral. Later, I found that it was not normal even for those early days in 1926.

The next morning I heard hammering in my father's shop, and since all field work had ceased, I had nothing to do and went down to the shop to find out what my father was doing. He was cutting 1" by 12" pine planks and making them into a coffin. He did this in just a few hours. He then brought it to the house and Mother lined it with some silky looking cloth and put a very small pillow at one end of the coffin. She had dressed Baby Ruth in a very pretty doll-like dress before laying her in the coffin. Then she called all of us children into the room so we could have a last look at Baby Ruth. Of course, we cried, all of us cried; we had lost our little sister. Then Papa placed two pine boards on the coffin, the same length of the coffin, and nailed them down. The coffin would never be opened again.

There was no church or funeral home service for Baby Ruth. Papa hitched two mules to the wagon and put the coffin in it. At the time we had a T-Model Ford. All of the family crowded into the car, a touring car with open sides, and rode to the cemetery where my father had bought a family plot. We waited until my father would have had time to get there, two and a half miles away, in the wagon. My oldest brother said he had wanted to ride with Papa to keep him company on the lonely ride to the cemetery, but Papa said he preferred to go alone. I guess he wanted nothing to interfere with his thoughts. He had buried two children years before, even before I was born.

The Baptist minister met us at the cemetery where a tiny grave had been prepared. A few close relatives and friends, mostly my mother's, were there. The minister made a few remarks. All I remember is bits and pieces which I heard at funerals hundreds of times later... "in my house are many mansions...I go to prepare a place for you...I shall come again and take you into my own...suffer the little children come unto me, for of such is the Kingdom of Heaven...lo, I am with you always."

That's the way it was—a plain pine coffin made by my father of boards he had on a shelf in his shop, a few remarks, a lowering of the tiny coffin into the ground and Ruth was gone forever. Yet her spirit lives with me still.

Her little grave is there with that of my mother and father and other family members, all close by. I still cry when I see that cemetery plot which is located under a huge, spreading oak tree, and I get a little bitter when I think sulfa and penicillin, which had not been discovered then, would have saved her life.

Chapter 4

THE TORNADO

That Sunday in May started out as a warm, lazy, partly-cloudy, sultry day, but it certainly didn't end that way. No one could foresee the catastrophe that happened.

We had not gone to church that day. In fact, we didn't go to church very much during the two years we lived in the house Grandmother White built for us near her huge home.

On days such as this Sunday in 1919, we spent most of the day out playing in the yard or throwing rocks or sticks at the frogs, turtles, and snakes in the small bayou that was only about 200 yards behind Grandma's house. Water remained in a slimy pool near the bridge which crossed the bayou even in the driest summer because of the overflow from the Artesian well which ran day and night down a small ditch from her home to the bayou.

It was about an hour after we had eaten one of Grandma's fine Sunday dinners that Hubert and I were playing catch in the yard while she and other family members sat on the screened porch in the shade. The ladies had small, round, hand fans made of some kind of bamboo and were gently fanning their faces, as it was so hot and still.

In a very startled manner, Mother, who was looking to the east across an alfalfa field which we farmed, toward a huge red barn used to house mules and hay, asked, "What is that large object falling in the field over there?"

Of course, we all stopped what we were doing at the time and looked. Down from the sky came a huge piece of tin roofing which was used on the roofs of most of the tenant houses on all the farms in the Delta. It just floated down like a leaf falls from a tree in the fall after a killing frost. It seemed so strange. Then within minutes, other strange things began to happen.

It suddenly got darker, but we began to see leaves by the hundreds falling, yet we lived more than two miles from any woods. Anyway, there was no wind blowing, making what we were seeing all the more odd. Then we began seeing twigs, and small limbs falling. One piece of string came falling out of the sky. But there was no wind, even then.

By this time we were not only puzzled; we were becoming scared. What could possibly account for what we were seeing happen?

My father, who was cutting some grass behind Grandma's house with a Kaiser blade, must have sensed what was taking place before anyone else. He dropped his cutting blade and hurried to the house.

When he arrived he said, "It is so dark to the southwest that I know there must be a tornado coming directly toward us. That's the only reason I can think of for all those objects to be falling from the sky. They must be sucked up by the whirling winds, pulled high into the sky in the center of the tornado and then thrown out to fall miles away. Everybody be ready to go inside when I give the word."

He then went to the south side of the house to be able to see the clouds to the southwest. In about five minutes he came back and told all of us to go to the center room of the house, that he could see the tornado coming but didn't know if it would strike Grandma's house or not, as it was still about three miles away whirling in a zig-zag course. We went inside as told, more scared than ever. Then all of us lay down near an inside wall. Two beds were pushed together and mattresses from other beds were quickly piled on top of the two beds which had metal frames. All of us, six or eight, lay down under the mattress-covered beds to wait. Papa said he would come back into the house just as soon as he knew whether the tornado would strike the house or not.

During his last look before coming inside to arrange the mattresses he said, "It looks to be about one-third of a mile wide and its funnel goes up to the clouds. It looks almost like a mushroom. It is moving slowly forward."

But of course, the whirling winds may have been going more than 150 miles an hour, fast enough to destroy any frame buildings in its path and to blow down any tree, no matter how large.

Just as Papa left the house an old Negro man named Mose, who worked for my grandmother, came to the back door and said, "Mister Ferguson, get me your double-bladed ax quick. I can stop the tornado from hitting us."

Of course, Papa didn't know what he meant and asked him why the ax would protect us from the storm.

Mose said, "I'll stick the ax in the block of wood out back of the house and the blade that sticks up will split the storm, sending half of it on one side of the house and the other half on the other side. It will be calm in the middle and we won't get hit by the winds."

Well, that was a new idea for the family to hear. But Papa gave him the ax, and with a mighty swing he embedded one blade of the ax in the oak block leaving the upper blade to deflect the storm.

I never knew whether the embedded double-ax blade affected the storm or not but within three or four minutes Papa came in and said it seemed to be turning west of the house and would miss on the west. A minute or two later he came back and said it was heading straight for Grandma's house. Still later, when we could even hear the noise it made, he came in and said it was going east of us for certain and we could get out from under the beds and watch it from the dining room window. I was just tall enough to see everything over the window sill and I still remember what a terrible thing I saw.

It was about three-fourths of a mile from our house to the edge of town, Moorhead, on the east. There was a tenant house on the south edge of the little bayou which ran behind Grandma's house. A Negro man, his wife, and a little baby lived there. About half a mile east was the huge barn we used to store hay in. This barn was on land my father farmed but did not own. Neither did my grandmother own it.

As the storm came nearer and nearer, the noise got louder and louder. I've heard people say a tornado sounds like about ten freight trains going by at the same time. The noise was truly fearsome and the clouds were down against the ground.

I was looking at the tenant house when the black cloud engulfed the house and I could see it no more. Then I watched the huge red barn. It looked large and strong and there were huge oak trees alongside the barn. How could any tornado blow such strong things down, I thought to myself. The black cloud moved forward and soon hid the barn and trees from view and then, in about one minute or maybe two, the tornado and all its noise moved on between us and Moorhead and was soon lost to view as it moved to the northeast. The huge barn and the large oak trees were swept away as if by a giant broom. Then the rain came; rain so hard that one could hardly see a hundred feet out to the road beside Grandma's house.

Moorhead escaped the storm, which passed between Grandma's house and the town, but the people in town must have known what took place because within half an hour people were coming out on the railroad, on foot, and on the gravel road in wagons and one or two cars driven by the two local doctors. By this time there were about half a dozen cars in the area. The doctors seemed to know what to expect and they had loaded medicine and bandages into their cars.

I never knew exactly why, but Grandma's house became an emergency treatment station. Within an hour or two wagons started arriving from the back country from the south. They were loaded with injured. Those who lost their lives were to be buried later. Right then the emphasis was on saving the injured. There were blacks and whites. Nobody paid any attention to who was black and who was white.

The little house on the bayou was swept away. Only stone steps were left after the storm. When the report came that the man and wife were killed, I started to cry and thought to ask, "Where is the baby?"

No one could find the baby and thought it must have blown into the muddy waters of the bayou. But just in case of a miracle, a search party began looking from the bayou, across the cotton field to the north. When the party was almost 200 yards from the house, but just before reaching the railroad which ran east and west (the C. & G.), someone thought he heard a baby crying. As they moved along, the cry became louder and louder, and then they found the baby. Its head and shoulders were lying on a row of cotton and above the water-filled furrows. The baby was on its back and screaming for all it was worth. The miracle was in its being carried over the water-filled bayou and 200 yards beyond, after which the violent storm had gently laid it down on its back. The baby did not have a scratch on it. Later, my mother said it was adopted by its aunt.

So many times since that day, I have wondered what happened to that baby in the storm. How high did the whirling wind take it into the sky? Was it completely naked before the storm as it was when found? It had to be the vacuum in the middle of the storm that sucked it up when the house in which it lived exploded outward. With all the sticks, stones, dirt, rocks, tree limbs and other debris whirling around above the earth, why was the baby untouched by anything? The storm hadn't taken its breath away and had laid it gently down where it wouldn't drown. I always guessed that only God knew how it all happened as nobody I knew ever told me.

The injured from the storm were treated by the doctors and laid on the mattresses which we had thought we would hide under to escape the storm. Some of those with broken limbs were taken in wagons to town where the doctors could put casts on their arms or legs. Others remained overnight. Grandma's house was full of people working to care for those that were hurt and offering comfort as best they could.

It was several days before the last of the injured were removed from Grandma's house, but she didn't complain. She just wanted to help if she could. Crews from town came out and helped rebuild some of the houses blown down by the storm.

It was only a day in the life of a five year old who was too little to be of much help, but it was a day he would always remember.

Chapter 5

TROUBLES WITH DOGS

The tornado was a big event in my life, but there was another event that was equally exciting even if it didn't affect as many people.

In the South there was a hideous disease that affected dogs during summer. It didn't happen very often, but when it did, lots of people became scared and wary of dogs that seemed to run aimlessly. These dogs got a disease known as hydrophobia, commonly known as rabies. In everyday language we thought of them as "mad dogs". They were really "mad" in that the disease affected their brains. They drooled at the mouth and began to run as the disease advanced. Sometimes they would run for perhaps twenty to twenty-five miles before they stopped and died. Just to think about such a death is pretty terrible, but the damage they sometimes did before dying was terrible too.

When they became diseased to the point that their brain was strongly affected, they would want to bite everything they saw move. Of course, they didn't know what they were doing but this made no difference to the person or animal bitten. The size of the victim made no difference, as they would bite horses or mules as well as other dogs or even cats.

We kids were always told that if a mad dog came near us and we knew it was mad, because of our having been warned, the thing to do was to stand stock still. My dad always said to pretend we were trees, as still objects did not attract mad dogs. He always said the dogs with rabies were insane and this caused them to be unaware of life if an object did not move.

Sometimes a mad dog would invade a school yard while the kids were out playing at recess. He would run from one to the other, biting each one that moved. Small kids could hardly be expected to have the nerve and courage necessary to be very still with a raging mad dog nearby. The first thought for any school child was to try to run to safety within the school building. Some were saved by doing this, but those bringing up the rear in a group trying to escape were often bitten.

Once this happened at the Moorhead Grade School and sixteen kids were bitten before they made it to safety. Neighbors hearing the commotion and screams of "mad dog" quickly got out their shotguns and killed the dog, but he had already done his damage.

On another occasion a mad dog got into the schoolyard of a black grade school. In those days black and white kids did not go to school together. There was segregation of the races in 1919 and the only time they mingled as if there were no color difference was when there was dire danger for everyone such as the time the tornado did such horrible damage. This Negro school was located on a gravel road about one and one-half miles south of Grandma's house. Two wagon loads of kids were bitten, that means about fifteen or twenty, or even more.

There was a cure for rabies if a person was bitten. The French scientist, Louis Pasteur, developed an anti-toxin that would prevent rabies if given properly. But the prevention was very painful in itself. Once a week all the kids who had been bitten came past Grandma's house in wagons on the way to the doctors in town where they were treated. The treatment required the use of a very long needle, long enough to go deeply into the patient's hip. It caused extreme pain but was absolutely necessary if a bitten person were to survive. All doctors said death from rabies was one of the most horrible deaths one could die. Some of those black kids were very small and two of the victims were teachers who tried to defend the kids by getting between the mad dog and the children. All were transported by wagon as there were no school buses, and too, the road was only a dirt road which became a loblolly after big rains.

The C. & G. Railroad ran along in front of Grandma's house, which was about one mile from the center of Moorhead. One day Hubert and I were on the railroad throwing rocks. It must have been a Saturday or Sunday, as Hubert was home from school; I hadn't started at that time. We were about 200 yards from the house when we heard yells in the distance. We stopped throwing rocks to listen carefully to the yells and faintly heard, "Mad dog, mad dog!" Of course, this was the yell that warned all to get inside with their pets and to put their horses in any barn that might be available.

Upon hearing the warnings we ran as fast as we could, but looking back we could see some men on horses coming along the railroad. Running in a straight line between the rails about a quarter of a mile away, we could see a pretty big dog but we couldn't tell what kind he was, whether a German Shepherd, a Collie, or some type of hunting dog, of which there were many around.

When we arrived on the porch, of course we yelled, "Mad dog," to anyone who was in hearing distance of us.

Visiting us was Uncle Earl, a plumber. He and Papa quickly made a plan as to how they would kill the mad dog and thus save others that might be in his path farther down the railroad. Papa had a ten-gauge shotgun loaded with buckshot, a very large shot normally used for deer hunting. There was no other suitable weapon around, but Uncle Earl grabbed a sledge hammer, about a six-pound hammer with a four-foot handle, which was used to split tree trunks and drive posts into the ground.

By the time they got outside they could see the mad dog about 200 yards away. He was running in a straight line, and as he got closer, they saw foam at his mouth. They ran off the front porch toward the railroad embankment in an effort to head him off. There was a ditch between the house and railroad that was about five feet wide and full of water. Uncle Earl threw the sledge hammer across the ditch and then jumped over it. Papa couldn't throw the shotgun over—he had to hold it and try to jump across. When he jumped, he didn't make it completely across and lost his balance. As he fell the barrel of the shotgun was pointed down and it stuck in the mud, plugging up the barrel. With mud in the end of the barrel it could not be fired without the barrel exploding and perhaps seriously injuring the person firing the gun.

By this time the dog was only about twenty-five yards away and when he saw their movement he headed straight to them. We were watching through the screen door. I've often wished we had not been looking. As the dog jumped toward my father, he could only swing the butt of the shotgun at the mad dog's head. The shotgun hit the dog's head squarely and foam from his mouth flew everywhere. This only knocked the dog down and he got up and headed for Uncle Earl who smashed him on the side of the head with the sledge hammer. This stunned the dog momentarily, and when he appeared to be almost unconscious, Papa jumped on his back forcing him to the ground, and Uncle Earl dispatched him for good with a blow of the sledge hammer to the top of the head.

By this time, the horsemen from town had caught up with the dog and saw the final action. That was one of the most exciting moments of my life.

One said, "Gilbert, why didn't you shoot the dog and not risk having him bite you when you jumped on top of him?"

"My gun barrel was plugged up with mud," he replied.

The horseman knew he had something to tease my dad about and said, "What a jumper! Can't even jump a little ditch like that without sticking his gun barrel in the mud, and then has to put that mad dog out of his misery with his bare hands."

The people in town teased my father about that for several years, but really, I know they admired him for what he did. I thought he was very brave.

I ask myself why I would want to tell a scary story like that. I guess it is because one should tell the bad things about growing up as well as the happy things. The other reason is that I had nightmares and dreamed about mad dogs for many years afterward. I always dreaded having one of those dreams.

Almost every farm family, whether black or white, had dogs around the house. Why they had them, I don't know. Most of them were not used for hunting dogs. I suppose the owners thought they would bark and warn them of intruders. But these dogs produced other dogs and, in those days, there were no dog pounds where strays were taken to be claimed as pets or put to sleep.

Lots of times, the owners, who didn't want a whole pack of dogs around the house, would take them far away and turn them loose in the woods. At that time, no more than one third of the land was in cultivation; the other was in swamps, woods, or canebrakes. These dogs, left to forage for their food the best way they could, became almost wild and, in some respects, they *were* wild, although they might be hiding and watching from thick bushes or underbrush.

Sometimes at night, they would slip out of the woods and go to someone's house to try to pick up some scraps of food that might have been thrown out and sometimes, if they got very hungry, they would raid the chicken houses and kill a few chickens for food.

Usually we would know when a wild dog or a chicken snake was in the chicken house by the noise the chickens made when they were disturbed while sleeping on their roosts at night. The chicken snakes would crawl in silently, find a chicken nest with eggs in it and begin swallowing eggs whole, without breaking them in any way. Snakes didn't seem to frighten chickens very much, but wild dogs were a different matter.

On this particular night, a wild dog came to our house, probably from the woods nearby, and I suppose he had nosed around a while and didn't find anything to eat. He didn't get into our chicken house, as the door had been fastened for the night.

It was summer and the nights were hot. Only the screen doors were closed, so that any night breeze that might come up would cool off the interior and make sleeping more comfortable. Most times, we latched the screen doors, but one latch made no difference; the one on the kitchen door. The screen in the bottom half of the door had been kicked loose by so many of us going in and out, and it was broken on one side. There was quite a bit of food on the table and on the stove, left over from supper.

This dog must have been pretty hungry, because he overcame his wildness long enough to slip through the hole in the door and noisily began eating a plate of biscuits on the stove. In the summer my father slept on a cot at the end of our combined kitchen and dining room. He awoke and heard the dog eating. After looking carefully, he could see the outline of the dog reared up against the stove.

As usual, Papa's ten-gauge shotgun was standing in a corner about ten feet from him. He jumped out of bed and yelled at the dog. This scared the dog out of his wits and he became disoriented and forgot where the door was. Instead of heading for the door through which he came, he headed through the house and through Mother's bedroom. In his fright he barked like I hadn't heard a dog bark before. He was as scared as we were.

By this time, my father had his gun loaded but the dog had gone through Mother's room, banged his head on her front screen door to no avail, then had run frantically into my room. Of course, his barking woke everyone in the house. I sat up in bed just in time to have him take a huge leap onto my bed and then into the window, which was open. Again, a screen repelled him, and this time he headed to my front screen door. This is one time I wished I had left the door unlatched because he crashed into it and bounced back.

All this happened within seconds. It was dark as pitch. We could only see the outlines of the dog and didn't even know his color. We just knew he was barking like crazy and we didn't know what to do.

He reversed his course, headed back through the kitchen, and at last, saw the screen door through which he had come. By this time, Papa was ready, and just as he went through the screen door, Papa fired. But in the dark he missed and shot off a part of the lower door. He rushed onto the small back porch to take another shot at the running dog. This time, he fired with dire results. What happened next was the cause of comments for years to come.

We had a rather large farm bell mounted on four posts beside the porch, which was off the kitchen. Mother could reach the bell rope from the porch and it was her job to ring the bell each work day at 11:30. The bell could be heard three-quarters of a mile away on the south side of our farm. She rang it again at 1:00 p.m., as a signal for everybody to go back to the fields. One of the posts of the bell support had just about rotted out and was in a weakened condition. It was just standing there lending almost no support for the bell, which was mounted about eighteen feet high.

As the wild dog ran past the bell post, my father shot at him again, but this time he hit one of the good bell posts, cutting entirely through it and leaving the upper half of it dangling uselessly in the air. Imagine what happened next. The huge bell began to topple onto the porch roof. It smashed down on it making more noise than it ever did when Mother rang it for the noon hour.

As you can well guess, the dog got away, but the fright of his life kept him from ever returning. The bell was not broken and we built a new platform for it very soon after. We kids didn't tease our father very much, but Hubert got up nerve enough to make fun out of my father's marksmanship on later hunting trips.

He would say such things as, "Papa, if we flush a covey of quail, you will probably shoot a tree down rather than bring down a quail." Or he would say, "Papa, now don't hit the bell posts," when he would be aiming at a hawk or something else. Papa would just smile faintly and bear the humor.

My being chased by bloodhounds came about accidentally, but it wouldn't have happened at all except for there being a county prison located only three miles east of our farm. This prison was for minor offenders such as unarmed burglars or bad-check writers. Most of the inmates were non-violent and were sentenced to no more than two years at most. Still, some of them couldn't be patient and serve out their short sentences and they attempted to escape from time to time. Usually, we heard about such escapes by word of mouth and not by radio as we had no radio and there were only a few around.

Escape was not so difficult in the first place, since the prisoners often worked outside the prison on roads, city, or county projects. They were not chain gang prisoners that the movies often portray. Each time I saw a group of them working I thought of how badly they must wish they were at home with whatever family they might have living on the outside.

If escape was fairly easy, recapture was pretty easy, too. The prison had a number of bloodhounds used in tracking escapees to their hiding places in a house, in the woods, or wherever. Tracking didn't always work, though, because a friend or relative would sometimes be waiting in a car on a lonely road or have a horse or mule tied to a tree in some secret spot. If the escapee could make it to the friendly car or horse, the blood-hounds would lose the scent and be helpless. Before tracking, these bloodhounds were taken to the scene of the escape or allowed to smell the convict's bedding. Once they got the person's scent they could track for miles. Experts say each person has his own distinctive scent just as he has his own fingerprint differing from all others.

I didn't know if it were true or not, but people said bloodhounds could be thrown off the track if the escapee would wrap his shoes or feet in some kind of cloth such as burlap and sprinkle the cloth with red pepper, black pepper or spices. These unusual odors were said to cancel out the person's natural scent. I can't vouch for the truth of that statement but I know bloodhounds got on my track one night and followed me about two miles, almost scaring me to death in the process.

One summer night, Saturday, I think it was, I had walked the Y. & M.V. to town to visit my friend, Franklin Spencer. Walking the railroad to town, about three miles, was nothing unusual. I did it many times. Franklin's family almost adopted me. My parents thought well of his family and I took vegetables from our garden to them many times. Being such good friends, I spent lots of nights at Franklin's house. This particular Saturday we planned to visit some girls who were together in one of the girls' home. We didn't really have dates because we were not old enough to call our get-togethers dates. We would just walk around town with the girls and buy them a treat of some kind, maybe an ice cream cone or a coke.

On this Saturday I started home about 10:30, walking the railroad. About one hour was required to make it home although I walked fast. Just outside of town the railroad passed through a large cypress swamp on a high embankment. At that point it was a little scary, with the huge trees towering over the railroad alongside the right of way. As this was near town and the railroad had a trestle offering some shelter from rain, hoboes quite often spent the night under the trestle. For this reason, I was always relieved when I got past the swamp into the country where open fields were along the railroad. On this particular night I was especially relieved as there was no moon out and it was almost pitch dark. But it was never too dark for me to see the rails on either side of the path I walked in the middle of the track.

When I was about two thirds of the way home, I thought I heard dogs barking far behind me on the railroad where I had already passed. At first I just thought they were farm dogs disturbed by an owl or something, but then I noticed lights, several of them, which seemed to be lanterns or flashlights. As the lights and dogs came closer and closer, I began to hear voices. Then it dawned on me that those dogs had the bark of a bloodhound. Most people don't know that a bloodhound does not bark naturally. They must be trained to bark and this prison trained theirs, since a barking dog is much more frightening to one being tracked than a silent one.

As the dogs got nearer and nearer, I knew I must do something to escape their path directly between the rails where I had walked. To the right of the railroad embankment was a Negro church and cemetery. Past the cemetery on the other side of a road lived the Gilliams, who knew our family. Although it was late at night I decided to head for the Gilliam home as fast as possible.

So off the railroad I went. First I climbed the chicken-wire fence around the cemetery and then stumbled through it, running into tombstones from time to time in the dark. Climbing the fence gave me a bit of headway as the dogs couldn't climb the fence and had to be lifted over. By the time they were crossing the cemetery, I was crossing the road in front of the Gilliams as fast as I could run.

I ran onto the Gilliams' porch and banged the door with my fist as hard as I could, while yelling, "Let me in, Mr. Gilliam, in a hurry, please!"

Mr. Gilliam came to the door and opened it just widely enough to shine a flashlight in my face.

"What in the world is the matter, Wilson? Are you in trouble or something?" he asked.

I said, "Mr. Gilliam, bloodhounds are chasing me. They are in the cemetery now and coming this way. I don't know why they are chasing me, but please let me in."

Mr. Gilliam opened the door, and locked it behind me.

Not more than thirty seconds later, as the dogs ran onto the porch, reared up on their hind legs and barked as if they had treed a coon or varmint of some kind.

There was a loud banging on the door and a harsh voice commanded, "Open up in the name of the law! This is the sheriff of Sunflower County."

Mr. Gilliam replied very nicely with his voice under control, "I'll open up when you call those dogs off. There's no need for them."

The dogs became quiet when ordered to do so by their trainer and Mr. Gilliam opened the door.

"What's the trouble, sheriff?" he asked, "Your dogs chased my neighbor across the cemetery. He's Mr. Ferguson's son and he's no escaped convict."

Then came a big surprise.

"We're not chasing an escaped convict. We're after a burglar who robbed the railroad depot tonight about nine. He broke open the cash drawer and made off with some money. We've chased him all the way to your front door and whoever went in your house must have done it. These dogs don't usually make mistakes," the sheriff said.

"Sheriff, you know good and well Wilson Ferguson wouldn't rob the depot. He doesn't get into that kind of trouble," Mr. Gilliam said in my defense.

"We'll see about that, friend. I don't know you, Mr. Ferguson, or his son. Let's have a talk with the boy," the sheriff requested.

I walked timidly out on the front porch and if it had been daylight anyone would have thought I was deathly sick because I would have looked as white as a bedsheet due to fright.

"What were you doing in town tonight, boy, and where were you about nine o'clock?" he asked in a gruff voice.

He didn't reassure me at all and probably still thought I was guilty. I explained how I had visited Franklin Spencer and some girls and had started home about 10:30.

"When did you start walking the railroad and where?" he asked.

I explained that I followed the sidewalk on Carpenter Street to the railroad and then turned south as I usually did. I knew the depot was four blocks north of the point where I got onto the railroad and I hadn't been on that four blocks of track at all that night.

"Well, maybe that clears things up for you just a little bit. We noticed the dogs were hot on a trail until they reached the crossing at Carpenter Street and then they milled around in confusion for a minute or two. Pretty soon, though, they picked up the trail hot and heavy and followed you to this house. The burglar must have had someone waiting in a car at the Carpenter Street crossing. This car picked him up and then the dogs struck your scent. Have you ever been in jail for any reason?"

I replied meekly that the only thing I knew about jails was what could be seen from the street and that I had never been accused of any crime in my life. By this time I was feeling just a little stronger and more confident. It seemed the sheriff was becoming more reasonable about the whole episode.

"Sheriff, those dogs scared the daylights out of me and they sure made a mistake," I said with some assurance.

"I believe you are right. Those bloodhounds must undergo further training. As it is, the burglar now has a two-hour headstart and it sure is going to be tough to catch him," the sheriff said in a kind of downcast tone. "Say, how far is it to where you live?" he asked.

"About half a mile," I replied.

"Boy, I believe I owe you a ride home. Jump in my car and I'll take you there," he offered.

I jumped in the car with him and during the few minutes it required to drive down the gravel road to my house we became better acquainted. He turned out to be a pretty good fellow, just "doing his job," as he explained.

The next morning at breakfast I had a startling tale to tell the family. At first they just couldn't believe I had actually been chased by bloodhounds, but when I told them about Mr. Gilliam and how he offered me safety from the chase, they knew I must be telling it pretty much like it happened.

Chapter 6

WHY I KNOW THERE IS A SANTA CLAUS

Each Christmas, newspapers print an editorial written many years ago in answer to a little girl's letter asking if there were really a Santa Claus. I don't remember exactly what the editorial says, but it reassures the little girl, whose name was Virginia, that there is indeed a real Santa Claus. It really doesn't matter what the editorial says as far as I'm concerned, as I know there is a Santa Claus and found out for certain at Christmas in the year 1919.

I had just turned five years old and had gotten to go to school as my birthday was in November rather than after January first. There was no kindergarten in those days so I went into the first grade.

We got out of school for the holidays a few days before Christmas, which seemed forever in arriving. The day before we got out, my mother popped enough popcorn to fill a five gallon can. This was my present to my class and everybody enjoyed the popcorn. Some of it was threaded with cranberries on string and hung along the schoolroom walls for decorations. When school was dismissed I took the strings home for decorations. People didn't use colored electric lights for Christmas in those days. Maybe they did in some large cities, but in small towns like ours, electric Christmas lights were not to be seen.

The rule in our home on Christmas Eve was that all kids had to be in bed by nine and asleep by ten. There were no exceptions among the six of us and getting out of bed was not allowed. That meant no peeping around corners to try to see Santa Claus when he put the gifts around the tree. But this Christmas was to be different; like no other Christmas in my life.

Two days before Christmas my father announced at our breakfast of hot oatmeal, fried ham, and biscuits with gravy, that he had a message from Santa Claus. Santa was going to visit our home in person Christmas Eve. What an event! He had never done that before and it brought up dozens of questions to say the least.

Visit our house? How could he get in? Our home was heated by an open fireplace. There was no way he could come down the chimney without getting burned and I quickly reminded my father of that.

"That is no problem. We can take care of that but it will require some work to get everything ready for him. We must move the woodpile in the back yard to the side of the smokehouse where we cure our ham and bacon, so that the back yard is clear. Oh yes, and we have to move the clothesline because the reindeer might get tangled up in it," said my dad.

We all pitched in and got the clothesline posts moved and the wood stacked. There didn't seem to be any question that Santa would arrive by sleigh. After all there were no large airplanes of any kind in those days and certainly no helicopters or jet planes. Sleighs haven't changed much over the years and neither have the reindeer's names. No doubt Santa has to retire some of his old reindeer from time to time but he just gives them the same names.

Of course, the plan was that Santa would land in our back yard but my dad said there was always the possibility he might land on a part of our roof that was pretty flat. Without anybody telling me, I knew right off that wouldn't work because the framework under that part of the roof was weak and certainly couldn't support eight reindeer, Santa, and a sleigh with tons and tons of gifts.

My father said, "Now we have the back yard clear, the roof clear, and everything ready except that we must remember to leave the kitchen door on the rear of the house unlatched so Santa can come in that way, because of the fire in the fireplace."

Our house was a very old, rambling, one story home with lots of rooms but no electricity or running water. The floors creaked badly in cold weather and it wasn't very warm. Between our kitchen and our living room was a large bedroom. Mother did all of her cooking on a giant-size, wood-burning range that also had a vat on one side in which we could heat about three gallons of water. We had four kerosene lamps for reading or studying at night. Being in the first grade, I had no homework to do, but the brothers and sisters older than I studied around the dining table, using two of the lamps and helping each other with arithmetic and spelling or whatever their assignments were. There were six of us kids at home that year, except that my oldest brother was in Memphis looking for a job. Memphis was in Tennessee about 150 miles north of our Mississippi hometown.

This Christmas Eve was the longest one I ever knew. I thought it would never end. Little questions kept popping into my mind all day.

One was, "Papa, are you and Mother going to bed tonight when we do, or what do you and Mother do?"

"Oh, I forgot to tell you that we all get to stay up tonight until Santa Claus comes to our house. After all, I want to see him just as badly as you do. I want to see what the old gentleman looks like," Papa said.

That answer left some faint questions in my mind but I didn't tell him what they were. After all, I was five and heard some of the older kids at school hint that my ideas of Santa Claus might just be all wrong. My older brother, Hubert, was one of those, but he didn't say much about my thoughts. He was going to get the shock of his young life just a few hours later, but it was still about five hours until dark. During those hours we put up holly branches and hung mistletoe over doorways. Holly and mistletoe grew in the woods nearby. There was no pine or spruce for Christmas trees growing in the Mississippi Delta country, so we used holly which had broad prickly leaves and clusters of red berries on each limb. Mother said she wanted to be sure to leave one kerosene lamp lighted in the big kitchen so Santa could see his way when coming in the back door, if indeed he did come. To tell the truth, I wondered if he were really coming to see us in person, but I wouldn't have expressed my doubt for anything.

Living across the street was Mr. Ware, a very good neighbor, and owner of the best grocery store in town. He was a large man, big around the middle, and had a booming voice. Mr. Ware always warned us boys to keep our hands off the big bunches of bananas which he had hanging from the ceiling of his grocery store.

He would always say, "Now boys, keep your hands off those bananas because a tarantula might bite you and they are very poisonous. When the bananas are shipped from South America, tarantulas sometimes hide in the bunches." You can be sure that was all he had to say.

About half an hour before dark, Mr. Ware, who had the only telephone nearby, came jogging across the street and said, "Mr. Ferguson, I just had a call from your oldest son, Morgan, from Memphis. He said to tell you that he couldn't get here for Christmas Eve because the train he was to come on had a breakdown in Memphis and he would be home on Christmas Day."

Mr. Ware, like any good neighbor, was always bringing us messages, and I began to wonder if he had given my father the message that Santa Claus was to visit us in person.

"By the way," he asked, "are you expecting Santa Claus tonight? Mrs. Spencer up the road said she saw you and the boys moving your woodpile and Mrs. Ferguson's clothesline."

"Yes," my father said, "we are expecting the old boy in person around nine or ten tonight."

"Great," Mr. Ware said, and they smiled neighborly smiles at each other as Mr. Ware turned to go back to his house.

After a seemingly endless day of waiting, darkness came. It was clear and cold and millions of stars came out brightly. The two end stars on the Big Dipper pointed straight to the North Pole from whence Santa was coming. Of course, he had to stop over in Alaska and Canada but I didn't have a doubt he was on his way. We ate an early supper and Mother noted that we were not as hungry as we usually were. No doubt it was the excitement we all felt, but no one would admit to that.

After supper, we unlatched the kitchen door, lighted one kerosene lamp which we left on the dining table as planned and went into the living room. It was about 7:30 and pitch dark outside. Papa picked up his daily newspaper, which came from Memphis, and read something about Santa having left the North Pole fairly early in the day. The article named the reindeer and he read their names to us. Mother picked up her sewing, which she always had plenty of, and began sewing by the table on which one kerosene lamp sat. The older kids got out a set of dominoes and started playing. When it dawned on them that there were only three to play with Morgan gone, Mother put down her sewing and joined them in a four person game with two playing against the others. I watched although I knew how to play. Of course, they didn't think I did. It was always the same, the big brothers and sisters just don't have much time or regard for how much the little ones know.

As time slid so slowly by, I just had to make conversation with someone. So I went over to Papa at his reading table before the fireplace and asked, "Papa, are you nervous about Santa Claus coming?"

He seemed so at ease that his answer startled me. "I'll say I am. I'm just as nervous and excited as you are. I can't even remember what I'm reading," he said.

I felt better knowing I wasn't the only one who was excited. I began to get sleepy, but each time I nodded as if going to sleep, someone nudged me in the ribs.

At ten it happened. How do I know it was 10:00? Because we had an old Seth Thomas clock on the mantel above the fireplace and it began to strike ten. As it finished striking we could hear a faint sound as if something was brushing our roof with a broom. What could that be?

"Don't get your hopes up yet," my father said, "remember we have some pigeons that are trying to make nests in our eaves."

Silence set in again and Papa picked up his paper to continue his reading, but he didn't read very long.

No sooner than he had started reading, we heard the kitchen screen door squeak. That door squeaked every time somebody opened it. There were two doors between the kitchen door and the living room where we sat. For a minute or two there was nothing but silence. All I could hear was my heart beating inside me. Not a word was spoken. Whoever wrote the Christmas poem and the lines that say, "Not a creature was stirring, not even a mouse," must have known what we were going through—that's how quiet it was. Papa dropped his newspaper; Mother put her sewing materials on the floor; the domino game halted, and we kids turned as white as sheets. I couldn't see myself, but I could see the others and felt sure I looked about as ghostly as they did.

Next, we heard footsteps, heavy footsteps as if they were carrying a load. They came to the second door and halted in the darkened room between the living room and kitchen. Everybody had forgotten about putting a lighted lamp in that room. Probably this mysterious visitor was lost for a minute and couldn't decide which door to open. He must have seen a faint light under the door to our living room because the door suddenly opened wide.

There in the doorway, as big as life itself, whatever that means, stood Santa Claus. His head was covered with a sort of stocking cap in red and white, his beard was long, white and flowing down to his chest, and he wore little granny glasses with small gold rims. He looked so tall and so big around. I remember him as if it were yesterday, although it seems I was in a state of shock.

His suit was red, trimmed in white, and he wore black boots of leather. Then came the first big "Ho! Ho! Ho! Merry Christmas to everybody! I've brought you a few Christmas gifts."

He began pulling out filled stockings from the sack and each had a name on it.

What the other kids got, I can't remember, because I was so in awe of having Santa Claus right there in our house, in person!

When he came over to me he asked, "Have you been a good boy?"

For the life of me, I can't remember what I replied or even if I had nerve enough to say anything at all. It's a mystery as to how Santa Claus knows certain things.

A big surprise came when he said, "It was pretty nice of you to take that five gallon can of popcorn to school this week. That shows the Christmas spirit—giving to others. The kids enjoyed Christmas a little bit more because of your gift."

I was so stunned that I couldn't remember to tell him that it was my mother's idea, that I would never have thought of the popcorn except for her.

What did I get from Santa? In my stocking was a new pocket knife such as all small boys want, an orange, an apple, some pecans, a few pieces of candy just like in Mr. Ware's store, and some English walnuts, which we never saw except for Christmas time.

When Santa got to Papa, I wondered if he had anything for him. Surely he did, but first he asked, "Gilbert, have you been a good father to this family this year?"

When my father said he had done his best, Old Santa handed him a stocking just like ours, but with his name on it. There were several little items such as a handkerchief, nuts and candy, but the main gift was a beautiful pearl handled straight razor such as all men used in the days before electric or safety razors were invented, the same kind barbers still use when they shave customers. My dad was overjoyed to get the razor.

Then Santa moved over to where my mother sat so quietly with a gentle smile on her face and her long hair all pinned up into a ball on the top of her head. Her stocking was very heavy and Santa reached into it and pulled out a flat iron. The iron was very smooth on the bottom, had a handle on top with which to grip it, and weighed about four pounds. Santa knew Mother heated the iron on the cookstove and after smearing a little beeswax on it, ironed our clothes.

When he had handed out all the presents, Santa Claus said, "Folks, it's going to be a long night and I must see lots of people."

Finally I got up nerve to ask him a question, "Santa, people say you have eight reindeer. What are their names?"

He replied, "I rest my reindeer and don't use the same ones each year, but their names stay the same. They are Dasher and Dancer, Prancer and Vixen, Comet and Cupid, and Donner and Blitzen. Pretty names, don't you think?"

So off he went with a big, "Ho! Ho! Ho!"

The next morning I looked carefully in the back yard to see if there were any tracks that could have been made by Santa and his sleigh the night before. At one spot there were imprints in the ground that could have been made by a stick with two prongs. They could have easily been deer tracks. Some of the grass seemed to have been nipped off in small patches and there were two marks on the ground that could have been formed by the runners of a sleigh, but my older brother said they may have been caused by planks being laid alongside each other in the grass. Of course, I didn't believe him and told him so.

So, I know there is a Santa Claus because I have seen him. He is as real as the human spirit and has been seen in Alaska, Norway, Sweden, Canada, and all over the world for that matter. It's too bad some kids never get to see the real Santa Claus, as I did. Many of them see the ones in stores and on the streets during the Christmas Season and that's okay, because they are supposed to represent the Spirit of Christmas. But that's not like seeing the real Santa Claus such as the one that came to our house so many years ago.

Chapter 7

WE BUY THE FARM

My father would have enjoyed being Daniel Boone's right-hand man, if I have him figured out correctly. He enjoyed the woods; he enjoyed clearing and planting land, and he enjoyed hunting. He seemed to always want to be on the edge of civilization or settled areas. I think that something closely akin to those likes prompted him to help hunt illegal whiskey stills in both Alabama and Mississippi.

So, when he saw an opportunity to buy a farm one and one half miles south of Grandma's big house, that only had about fifty acres out of 160 acres in cultivation, with 110 acres of trees and underbrush, he jumped at the opportunity. This was in 1921 when I was only seven and buying a farm didn't mean all that much to me.

By this time we had grown to be a family of eight. There were our parents, oldest brother Morgan; oldest sister Clara; older brother Hubert; me, Wilson; younger brother Louis, who was born while we lived near Grandma; and Paul, also a younger brother born during the short time we lived in Moorhead in the house where I had met Santa Claus in person. Kathleen, Imogene, Ruth, and Fred were born after 1921. Fred was the last of twelve kids Mother bore, as fast as nature would allow. Mother's first child was born in 1905 and her last one in 1927, the year of the great flood in the Mississippi Delta.

But where could Papa get the money to buy the farm when money was so hard to come by? Later, he told me where. He knew his father was a reasonably prosperous farmer and circuit rider Baptist minister. He had ridden his horse to small churches located in the hills for miles around and it may be that those church goers contributed quite a bit to his earthly savings while he was building his favor in Heaven. Whatever the reason, Papa said that he asked for one thousand dollars from his future inheritance to be used in buying the farm down in the Mississippi Delta. Grandpa agreed and gave him one thousand dollars in gold, for which Papa bought a very secure money belt to be used in carrying the money 250 miles to Moorhead. Papa traveled by train on the famous C. & G. Railroad as there was no other transportation.

Papa made the deal for the farm when there was only one house on the 160 acres. It was an old, almost square, tenant house occupied by a family of Negroes who farmed the land for the white owner before Papa bought it.

So, in 1921 Papa and my two older brothers began building our home, and in 1922 we moved into it. It was finished, but it was pretty plain. The house was built of pine lumber with no heating system except for a double fireplace located between the two front rooms. There were four rooms with a long, wide kitchen attached to the back. How could six kids and two adults live in a four room plus kitchen house? Easy, I guess. There were two beds or two beds and a cot in every room. There was a bed or cot in one end of the kitchen all the years I was growing up. Our house had no running water, no electricity, no insulation, and no storm windows. It was not painted, and at first, the floors were bare except for deerskin rugs. These skins had bullet holes in them. Wood was our entire source of heat for warmth and cooking.

A big day in my mother's life was when Papa bought her a huge Garland Range wood cookstove. One could heat water in a compartment beside the firebox and we did many, many times for our baths. Baths we had to take!

As Mother always said, "We may be poor but we will be clean."

And we were. In summer, we sat a tub of water out in the sun so it might become warmer for a bath just before bedtime. These baths were taken in zinc tubs. In winter the tub was placed near the kitchen cookstove which had a fire in it most of the time.

Or course, there were no inside sanitary facilities. Our toilet was an outdoor privy located about seventy-five feet from the kitchen door. It was a two-holer. We boys got quite a kick, and reprimands, for throwing a small stick of stove wood against the thin, pine walls of the privy when our younger sisters were occupying it. Of course, they yelled at the top of their voices as the stick of wood banged against the privy. Just imagine it and one can understand.

Our furniture was fairly plain. We had iron bedsteads, straight chairs for the most part, with cane bottoms, and one or two rockers for our parents. The kitchen table had so many leaves that we could extend it for twelve people, if needed. There were a few pictures, one of them being the capitol building in Washington. Our source of music was a gramophone which one would wind up tightly before putting a record on to play. After years of effort its spring broke one sad day and there was no way to repair it. Except for the gramophone, the only music I ever heard at home occurred once when I came home from college. My two younger sisters, Kathleen and Imogene, who were in grade school at the time, and my mother were singing a trio while doing dishes. Their voices blended so perfectly. When they finished I asked them to sing some more but they wouldn't because I had made them self-conscious. I remembered their singing long afterward.

It was years after we built the house that we got our first radio and it, like most of the them in 1929 or 1930, was powered by a battery. One turned three knobs until they were all in a certain alignment before the Memphis announcer at WMC could be heard. Static was just terrible and it seemed every time one looked forward to the news or a ball game, a thunderstorm on the horizon made it impossible. We had no radio when Lindbergh flew across the Atlantic alone in 1927. It was such a big event that I persuaded my father to let me walk the three miles to town to hear it reported on one of the three radios in town. This one was located in the hardware store. It was so exciting to hear the announcer say that by wireless it had been reported that the Lone Eagle, as he was called in those days, had crossed Ireland and instead of landing in London, had continued on to Paris. When he landed in Paris to capture the twenty-five thousand dollar prize for the flight, mobs of happy, welcoming people almost overran his plane before police could hold them back.

One might ask how we preserved food for such a large family. It wasn't easy. Mother canned hundreds of Mason jars of vegetables from the garden which covered about half an acre. The only beef we had was fresh beef when a neighbor or we butchered a small calf. This was because we couldn't can beef. We always had our own pork which could be cured by immersing it in salt or smoking it. Of course, it was necessary to buy our staples such as flour, but we always had two milk cows and a fresh supply of milk. On special days we bought ice from a Model-T Ford ice truck that made a scheduled route two days a week. This ice delayed the milk from turning sour and perhaps once a month was used to freeze ice cream.

After building the house, we needed a barn quickly to house our seven mules. A different shelter was used for the cows. Papa sometimes seemed to think his mules were more important than his kids, or so it seemed to me. This may have been partly true because without mule power no cotton, corn, or soybeans could have been raised, as tractors to be used for cultivation were unheard of in the 1920s.

In those 1920s, I was too young to understand lots of things regarding families and was too timid to ask personal questions. For example: my mother's parents and grandparents were rather wealthy people and so were my father's. They were prominent people in their communities. So, why did Mother and Papa have nerve enough to go out on their own, live in a rather primitive manner, work like slaves for years (the kids did also), and do all this in a cheerful manner? I never knew the answer but their background must have had something to do with it. Certain rules were lived by. We were not allowed to use incorrect English. (Older kids further along in school always corrected incorrect English if we spoke it.) We were never allowed to even say, "Mother, you burned the eggs." The same rule prevailed regarding anything she cooked. Neither did Papa criticize her. Mother never seemed bitter even when she did not receive an inheritance she was due because it was spent by a younger, spoiled brother in his riotous living racing around the country in one of the first expensive automobiles that came to the area.

School was a must even if we couldn't start with the other kids in September, when we were needed so badly to pick cotton. We attended the first day, bought our books, and usually missed the first three or four weeks, but we had to study at night regardless. This was done around kerosene lamps placed on the kitchen table. If any rainy day prevented our working in the fields, we went to school that day. In our area the road to school became gumbo mud in winter, but if the school bus (a modified Model-T Ford) could not run due to  to bad roads, we just saddled up mules or rode bareback to school. Those mules never failed to make it. That's the way it was on the farm we bought in 1921 and it sounds like a dull, uneventful life that we led. But there were the good times such as the fish and ice cream suppers, the hunting trips, the camping expeditions, and seining trips. Anyway, although we knew nice things were hard to come by, we didn't feel like we were either poor or underprivileged.

Of what do kids, ages ten to seventeen, daydream about now days? Or do they daydream at all?

When I catch my grandsons staring off into space with their eyes seemingly focused on nothing, I ask, "What are you dreaming about? Or what are you thinking about?"

The answer is always, "Nothing," as they bring their thoughts back from space or some place else.

Well, I don't believe that answer. I think they are dreaming of something or fantasizing about being a famous athlete, astronaut, or doctor, or something which to them seems worth wishing silently for. As for girls, they have probably changed in their daydreams since the days of my boyhood more than boys. In the 'twenties girls always were dreaming of being nurses, teachers, or housewives, but now that opportunities have opened up for them, no doubt they daydream of being surgeons, astronauts, engineers, or lawyers just as the boys do. Given their boundless imaginations they may, in fact, dream more than the boys. Some no doubt still think of being nurses. It just doesn't seem natural to me for a teenager, or kids even younger, not to daydream of something they wish to be or do in the future.

In my youth, while on that Mississippi Delta cotton farm, there wasn't much to inspire ambition on the part of my brothers or me. Without running water, electricity, or even a battery radio until I was sixteen or so, there was seemingly nothing to look forward to. But look forward we did, even if it was pure fantasy, and my daydreams were a succession of thoughts which changed according to how old I was.

It was easier for me to daydream while working alone doing such things as plowing cotton, hoeing cotton, or doing the churning with an old churn with a plunger to push up and down while I read a book. Sometimes I would become so engrossed with the book that the churning was completed with all the butter having risen to the top of the churn.

At such times Mother would say, "Wilson, get your eyes out of that book and gather that butter in the churn."

Gather meant that I was to use a wooden paddle and push the globlets into larger balls of butter, finally ending with a pound or two of butter in one large glob.

In those days I became infatuated with cowboy and western stories. I got the Western Story magazines from either my uncle or aunt as my father wouldn't have allowed us to buy such "trash." He called them trash but I never knew him to read one. Of course, such stories encouraged me to want to be either a cattle baron or cowboy out west—probably one of the silliest ideas I ever had. I became so infatuated with western stories that I began to hide them between mattresses on my bed. Worse than that, my grades at school suffered so that the teacher wrote my mother a note saying she couldn't understand what had happened to my desire to perform well in school. Finally, Papa put a stop to the whole idea by banning western stories from the house and you can be sure I didn't violate his wishes on that score. As a result, my desire to be a western range man evaporated into thin air in about nothing flat. Another result was that my grades rose to normal in about a week.

My next big daydream grew out of a railroad crossing our farm. It cut off about one-fourth of our farm to the north and three-fourths to the south. There was one tenant house on the north side of the railroad, three tenant houses and our house on the south. A public gravel road ran between our house and the railroad.

Most young people have seen steam locomotives only in the movies, western movies that is, but we saw them every day. About two passenger trains and four freight trains passed within 125 feet of our house every day. If not busy in the fields, we kids lined up along the right of way to wave at the engineer, who always waved back. I've often wondered how he could wave at everybody up and down the line for more than a hundred miles.

When they passed our house, the trains were traveling about thirty-five miles an hour, maybe forty, with the coal car, which was a part of the locomotive, rocking back and forth. This rocking motion caused some of the lumps of coal to fall off alongside the tracks. We picked up the coal in gunny sacks from time to time and always had plenty to burn in my father's forge in his shop, where he heated and sharpened the plows we used on the farm. We boys had other plans for the coal, too. We sometimes held out on Papa and would use some of the coal to build "campfires" on the edge of the railroad at night, all the while pretending that we were out west on the range or on a camping trip in the woods.

Once Mother gave us permission to cook some crayfish tails in a pan on the fire. At the time we had never eaten shrimp, but we knew about it, and thought the crayfish tails would taste like shrimp. They didn't taste like the shrimp we imagined, but did taste strongly like acrid coal smoke. Also, they had a gritty taste as if sand was mixed into the meat. To this day, I don't know if we accidentally mixed sand in the lard we cooked them in or if they really do taste like that. Whatever the reason, we never cooked crayfish again.

That railroad and that waving engineer occupied my daydreams for a couple of years at least. Those big locomotives were powerful, with three huge drive wheels on each side. They belched black smoke most of the time and pulled as many as fifty freight cars. Today's modern diesels require as many as four engines to pull a long freight train, but I never saw more than one steam locomotive pulling an entire train in our flat delta country.

As our farm was fairly near town, the trains sometimes stopped in front of our farm to give time for other trains to clear the crossing of the C. & G. and the Y. & M.V. in Moorhead, three miles up the line. That's when we got to see the trains close up. What a thrill it was to walk alongside those huge locomotives that made us feel ant size. As they sat waiting with steam pressure up they constantly gave off a "chu-chug," "chu-chug" sound. What caused that noise I never knew because the engine wasn't moving. If the steam pressure in the boilers got too high the engineer could open a valve and the steam then escaped in a blast not unlike the blast from a modern-day jet engine on an airplane. It gave off a fearsome sound and we always kept our distance to be sure the steam jet didn't get near us. With a long train and a heavy load, when the engineer turned on his power those huge drive wheels would often spin very fast for several turns before the engineer could stop them. This was somewhat like an automobile spinning its wheels in snow or mud. But the engineer had a cure for that. He had tanks of fine sand mounted on the sides of the locomotive and allowed a tiny trickle of sand to fall on the rails in front of the drive wheels. Then when he turned on the power, the engine had traction with the sand preventing the wheels from spinning. The train began to move, the engine puffed steadily and the whole train picked up speed.

All this I had seen, but it didn't begin to match the day the train stopped, the engineer stepped down from his lofty perch in the cab, and came down to speak to me. I guess he had plenty of time to waste, but I know he must have been a fine fellow. He asked my name and said he saw me about three times a week. This was almost like talking to a famous athlete or movie star. Finally, I got up nerve to ask him if I could climb up to his cab and see the levers and gauges he used to run the locomotive.

He hesitated a bit and then said, "Yes, but I must help you up and be up there with you."

The steps were too far apart for me but he boosted me up somewhat like having someone boost me onto the back of one of our mules.

What a sight! The firebox door was open and the roar of the flames was almost deafening. The fireman was stoking the fire with shovels of coal to build up heat and steam for the time they would pull out. There were steam gauges, water gauges, speedometers, and other gadgets I didn't know enough to ask about. And then there was a lever which he moved when he wanted the train to go forward and backward. Also, there was the steam brake, which had so much power that it could lock those huge wheels when a quick stop was necessary.

I wanted to be an engineer more than ever. I asked him how I could plan such a career. He said all engineers had to start out as apprentices and ride the trains so as to learn all about the engines as well as all about the dozens of different signals up and down the line. He said he doubted I would have much of a chance to be an engineer unless our family were to move to Memphis where most of the engineers lived. If there, I could put in an application early and get into the apprenticeship program. He was as nice as could be, but I knew right off the bat that such a move was an impossibility. I might just as well have said I wanted to be a man on the moon. Little would I have thought there would ever be a man on the moon.

Although thrilling in itself to be in the cab of a powerful locomotive, the experience and the conversation put a quick end to my daydream of being a railroad engineer.

Chapter 8

DELTA OUTDOORS

Snakes of many kinds lived in the Mississippi Delta where we lived, and it was advisable to wear boots of some kind when hunting, although we didn't do so except if we were planning on walking in water while hunting. Then we wore waterproof rubber boots. This was usually only in winter, when the snakes, both moccasins and rattlesnakes, were in hibernation in hollow logs or holes in the ground. Then, we didn't worry about them.

It was in summer that they were to be feared, as they were out of their holes and moving from place to place. Most of this movement was at night, when they were searching for insects, mice, or small frogs. Of course, a large snake could swallow a large frog and swallow a fairly large fish as well.

We seldom saw rattlesnakes; they were wily creatures, usually staying around logs or patches of briars or bushes in the woods. But I have one rattlesnake in mind that, but for some good luck on my part, would have put me in the hospital.

Let me start with an explanation.

We heated our house with open wood-burning fireplaces and my mother did all her cooking on a large stove that was also heated with wood, which had to be cut into small sticks. Wood cutting was a big job because so much wood was required for heating and cooking. Most of the wood was cut in summer, giving it time to dry out so that it would burn readily in winter. We had lots of wood on our farm and we cut our own trees for wood, unless a neighboring farmer wanted some land cleared up for cultivation. When this happened, we cut and used his wood, thus saving our supply.

One summer day, after it had rained so much we couldn't work in the fields, my father and I took our axes, saws, and wedges with which to split logs, into the woods to cut fireplace wood. Along went my father's old ten-gauge shotgun. Why we took it I don't know, but it was always along in case of some kind of emergency. I found out what an emergency was that particular day.

Have you ever seen a cross-cut saw? If not, it is about seven feet long, has handles on each end and its teeth, which grind up the wood and make a furrow in it, are along one side of the seven foot length. Wood is cut by two people, one at each end, pulling the saw back and forth across the log. But, that is after the tree is cut down and is lying flat on the ground. First, we had to cut the tree down.

We picked a certain oak, which had few branches, and could be easily cut into lengths about two and a half feet long, after which the length would be split into quarters for the fireplace. After picking this tree, my father got on one side and I on the other with the saw between us. We began pulling the saw back and forth, parallel to the ground.

Every few minutes we would stop for rest, allowing the saw to remain in the slit it had made, and standing erect to rest our backs, arms and shoulders. Once, while resting with our feet in place, as they had been while sawing on the tree, I noticed my father looking at the ground behind me. What took place then is printed indelibly in my memory.

"Wilson, be perfectly still and don't move either of your feet, by all means," he said, "just stand there as you are standing now."

"What's the matter?" I asked.

"There's a rattler within six inches of your right heel and he's coiled to strike. He hasn't rattled yet, so he must not be really mad. When he rattles, that will mean he is ready."

My dad began to ease away, reminding me to be as still as a tree trunk. He went to a nearby tree for his shotgun. Out of the corner of my eye, I could see him pick up the gun and pump a shell into the chamber. Then I heard it: that buzzing rattle that only a rattlesnake can make when he is rattling his rattles by shaking his tail so fast that one can't see the movement of it. Each little bony rattle is connnected to the other and one more rattle grows each year. A rattlesnake with eight rattles is eight years old. I just couldn't resist turning my head to the right and downward, so as to see the snake. Maybe that is what angered him and started him rattling at me. He was coiled tightly, with his diamond shaped head pointed directly at my right heel. His long red tongue snaked out in anger and his rattling continued. There was really no reason to ask me to stand still—I was so frightened that I don't think I could have moved. If I had moved he could have struck my leg and imbedded his fangs in it, along with his deadly poison.

My dad approached very quietly from behind the snake. When about ten feet away, he aimed and fired directly at the rattler's head, which disappeared in a mass of blasted leaves and dirt. You can believe the blast of dead leaves, knocked against my leg, spelled relief from a few of the most anxious minutes of my life. We cut off the seven rattles the snake had and decided we had enough excitement for the day.

When we got home, Mother was cooking supper and asked, "What happened today? I thought I heard your shotgun," she said.

"Oh, nothing. I just took a shot at a varmint I saw in the woods today," my father replied.

He just said this because Mother was always worrying that a tree would fall on us or something else befall us. I guess the last thing she would have thought of was that a rattlesnake and his deadly poison had been so near my right heel.

One day, in the late fall of the year after frost, when leaves were becoming dry and falling from the trees, my father came in and announced that there was a peg-leg coon in the woods to the south of our farm. He had walked through the woods and had seen coon tracks beside the water. There were three separate tracks and then a small, round indentation in the ground where the other track was supposed to be. This old coon had been caught in a steel trap, which had cleanly snapped off one foot. The stump healed and then he just went on about his business of searching for his food. I imagine he may have been handicapped to some extent, but I can just picture him using his other front paw, slashing at minnows or crayfish, which strayed near the edge of the stagnant ponds found in low spots in the woods.

In those days, we were hunters, and hunting was one of our exciting endeavors. So it was only normal that my father would want to catch old Peg-Leg. Too, the fall of the year is the time to hunt for coons, as they are fat after eating persimmons and other things which grew in the woods. There was nothing better to us than barbequed coon. Our family had two hunting dogs, known as Walker Hounds, which were supposed to be good coon dogs. The neighbor also had two. All of us, perhaps ten people, went hunting for old Peg-Leg one night. There had been many hunts before, but the dogs had never picked up Peg-Leg's scent on any of those earlier hunts. This night was to be different.

We set out on a clear moonlit night. The bright moonlight might have been no advantage to the coon, but it was to us trying to make our way through dense brush, vines, bamboo cane and trees. No lights were allowed. The dogs hunted freely ahead.

In these woods, there were several towering oak trees, but there was so much dense underbrush, that I wondered how in the world the dogs could do anything with a coon, as quick as they are, in case they came upon one. Sometimes, when coons ran up a large tree, there were only two ways to get them. One was by waiting until day-light and then shooting them down when they could be seen. Waiting until daylight and then cutting the tree down was the other. It was sometimes possible to shoot the coon out of the tree at night by using a flashlight and having his eyes "shine" back. I suppose that is really a reflection of light, but almost all boys or girls have seen how a cat's eyes glow in carlights along dark roads at night. So it was with coons. They would sometimes look at the light and thus give their hiding place away. Papa had said before the hunt that old Peg-Leg would not look at the light and have the reflection of his eyes give his position away in a tree. He thought old Peg-Leg too smart to do that.

Time proved him right. After about an hour, suddenly the dogs began to bark that special-sounding bark that lets their owner know they have a fresh scent. They were moving at a fast pace, too. We followed as best we could, getting scratched by briars and vines as we chased the dogs. The dogs were getting almost too far away, when the tone of their bark changed. Now, they were barking at a still lower tone, with the sound coming from deep in their throats. Even I knew what that meant. They had "treed" the coon. We knew that even before we got to the tree, but when we did arrive, all out of breath and hot and excited, the dogs had the base of the tree surrounded and were barking a loud chorus, letting us know they had chased the coon up the tree. We knew it was a coon, because a possum could not have run as fast as the dogs did in their frantic chase. It looked like the old coon beat them to the safety of the tree by a very small margin. Of course, all this time, we thought it was Peg-Leg, but this was most likely because we wanted it to be him.

This oak tree was one of the largest in the woods, being about five feet in diameter and having huge limbs which extended outward maybe forty feet or so. These low-hanging limbs turned out to have a real meaning to Mr. Coon.

The flashlight was hauled out. It was a strong one with three batteries and rare in those days. My dad began to shine the flashlight up the tree and into the crotches, where the limbs joined the main trunk of the tree. Then, he turned the light out on the limbs. All this was to no avail, as Mr. Coon wouldn't look at the light and reveal where he was hiding. The light would not reach the very top of the tree, which rose perhaps eighty-five feet above the ground.

What should we do? The decision was easy. We would make beds of leaves, build a fire so the coon would know we were still there, thus thwarting his slipping cunningly down the tree, and wait until daylight, when we could see him.

We were exhausted from the hunt and thirsty, but the jug of water brought along for such an eventuality quenched our thirst. My bed of leaves felt very good, as they were recently fallen and were crisp and crunchy. So I went to sleep almost immediately in a warm bed of fallen oak leaves. My father said he would stay put and take turns watching the tree with my older brother, who also went to sleep.

What about the dogs? They were tired. They quenched their thirst in a very small pond of water, which was almost under the end of the longest of the low hanging limbs. Then they too went to sleep. So, everything was quiet, except for the normal night noises, such as a lone hoot owl, who was hooting in a nearby tree as if he had lost his mate and was heartbroken. After an hour or two, my older brother relieved my father at the watch post, but as you might expect he soon fell asleep while sitting up, using a small pecan sapling as his back support.

As for Mr. Coon, he must have been watching us with cunning thoughts as to how he might escape. Most likely, he had been in this situation before and knew from experience what to do.

I'll never forget what happened next, but at the time, I was confused, just like the dogs and everyone in the hunt. Suddenly, we heard a crashing noise in the brush and leaves out near the end of one of those long overhanging limbs. This awoke the dogs, who began barking loudly and running frantically in every direction, except toward the coon, it seemed. My dad awoke almost as soon as the dogs, and so did all of us.

Finally, we got the dogs pointed in the right direction by taking them to the spot where the coon had jumped from the branch to the brush below. The coon had taken about three jumps in one direction, and then turned suddenly left, splashing water the entire length of a small pond. The dogs did not make the turn as the coon had moments before. They kept on a straight line and lost the scent nearby. Of course, by this time the coon had made good his escape. He had outwitted all the hunters and the dogs. I will always remember the confusion and the milling around that erupted when the coon took his jump to freedom.

How did we know it was old Peg-Leg? The evidence was all there. When he took his first jump through the mud and out of the pond, there were three distinct paw prints and one round indentation, where the peg-leg had made its mark in the mud.

I didn't say it aloud (what boy of twelve would), but I was glad old Peg-Leg escaped. We never heard of him again, and I have always hoped he lived to a ripe old coon's age.

Except for our chances to go hunting in late summer and early fall, life was pretty dull and work became drudgery on our farm in the middle 1920s. In the Mississippi Delta, hunting squirrels was a great sport, ranking right alongside the hunting of rabbits, quail, coons and possums. And everyone agreed that Mother could really cook young squirrels, either by frying or stewing them, so that they were irresistible.

Hunting for coons and possums was done at night with lights and dogs. The lights were used to "shine their eyes" and dogs were used to chase them up trees, but squirrels were hunted in broad daylight when they could see the hunter, in most cases, before the hunter saw the squirrel. To be successful in hunting squirrels one had to know how to move through the woods as quietly as the Indians did. The crack of a breaking dry stick or the crunch of a foot on dry fallen leaves could be heard by a squirrel long before the hunter could get within shooting distance. Hubert and I had practiced moving through the woods without noise many times. We did this by one of us slipping up on the other, with the hunted having his eyes closed. We could have approached a "city boy" within ten feet without his knowing a living person was nearby.

The best squirrel hunting time was early in the day when the leaves on the ground were still moist and pliable from overnight dew, and before the wind came up. Even a light wind made a moaning sound in the tree limbs high above the ground and prevented our hearing squirrels bark when they sensed that they were being hunted. Also, early in the morning was feeding time for squirrels who ate buds, small acorns, wild pecans, or hickory nuts. After feeding they came down to the ground for a drink of water and then climbed their "home" tree for a noon nap before returning to feeding in the afternoon.

Our farm had about sixty acres of woods but we had hunted in them many times and had gotten tired of hunting so near home. To the southwest was a huge forest that was about four miles wide and many miles long from north to south. We called this forest the "deep woods" and were always asking Papa to let us hunt in the "deep woods."

There was a certain mystery about the "deep woods." Only a few years before, there had been bear killed in those woods and many thought there were bear still there. Of course, we never knew if the bear rumor was true or not, but we did know that when plowing with mules near those deep woods the mules always wanted to avoid the side of the plowed field nearest the woods. Old timers said mules and horses could smell bears and were deathly afraid of them. Horseback bear hunters often had their mounts rear and buck them off and head for home at breakneck speed when they smelled bears.

There was another rumor that was probably more true than false making the rounds regarding the "deep woods." Several plowmen, when working near the "deep woods," said they had heard the scream of a panther late in the evening. Everybody knew there were panthers in some of the Delta woods but no one knew for certain about any panthers being in the "deep woods." As for me, I had no doubts they were there, because Joe McMillan, a black man who worked on our farm, said he had heard the panther scream several times. When I asked him how it sounded he never could make a sound that could possibly resemble a panther, but he said it sounded about a hundred times louder than a cat screams when being hurt. He said it certainly wasn't like a cat's meow.

Even with all the rumor, Hubert and I were not afraid to hunt in the "deep woods," but I knew without doubt that neither of us had the nerve to hunt there alone. Such a possibility didn't exist in the first place since we were not allowed to hunt alone ever because of the danger of an accident.

I never knew what caused Papa to give us permission to hunt the "deep woods" but one surprising day he did. We were to go on the next Saturday when we were out of school.

On Friday night after getting home on the school bus we began making preparations. Guns were checked out and oiled. Hubert was to take the twelve-gauge-pump gun that held six shells, which meant that he could shoot six times without reloading. I was to take the twelve-gauge, full-choke, single-shot, hammerless shotgun. This meant I had to reload each time I fired it. Also, with its full choke and slightly longer barrel, it kicked much harder when fired than Hubert's. We had knapsacks with pockets, some to hold ammunition, and large ones to hold any squirrels we killed. Also, we wore rubber boots which weren't all that good for walking, but which were to guard against snakebite below the knee and to wade across the many shallow pools of water found in the woods. Hubert had a $1.50 Ingersol watch which he was to take as well as a compass, which only weighed about three ounces. Mother fixed up some sausage and biscuit sandwiches for our lunch.

About four on Saturday morning we rolled out of bed and gathered all our supplies. Papa had checked us out, and because the weather report in the Memphis *Commercial Appeal* the day before had predicted a clear day, we left the compass at home. As we had been trained by experience we knew we could not get lost because of our tracking of the sun during the day. We knew the sun rises in the east and is at its highest point (zenith) at noon and sets in the west. We also knew we were entering the woods from the north and intending to hunt in a southerly direction. With a com-pass we would have followed the indicator needle south, adjusting for any side trips we made, then reverse ourselves following the needle indicator north when we were ready to quit hunting. But because of the weather report, Old Sol himself was to be our compass as he made his way across the heavens from east to west; that is, Old Sol and a $1.50 watch.

So, as daylight was breaking, but before the sun came up, we climbed through the barbed wire fence lining the border of the "deep woods" and began our hunt.

Hubert said, "Wilson, we must watch for the sun to come up through the trees so we know which direction is east."

"Okay," I said, "we must both watch for the first sun rays."

From what reports we had heard, we must walk about two miles through the woods before we came to a large area of huge trees, so large they shut out the sun's rays, and the ground below the trees was free of underbrush. This was squirrel country. But first we must get there.

With our guns and extra gear to carry, we got tired after about one mile of walking through woods that had heavy underbrush, making our progress slower than we had expected. As we approached one of the many ponds we were crossing we decided to rest and have a drink of water. Our gear and guns were laid down on a large log that extended out into the pond of stagnant water. Up to this point we hadn't worried about making noise as we were not really in good squirrel hunting territory. By lying down across the log and brushing the algae away we drank from the pond. We were careful to be sure no tadpole was swimming near when sucking up the water from an upside down position. Drinking water in this fashion was common to us. No doubt we drank lots of bacteria not meant for man nor beast, but I don't think we ever drank any that were harmful.

We had hardly finished drinking, when we heard a scurrying sound in the woods near the edge of the pond. What a surprise! A mother coon and four baby coons were making their way to the water, both to feed and to drink. Coons at play are even more fun than kittens chasing a ball of twine. The tiny coons would run out into the shallow water and then turn around in fright and run back to the shore. They splashed water and wrestled each other in the water until wringing wet.

Then we noticed what the mother coon was doing. She moved slowly and gracefully on a dead log, all the while her eyes intent upon the water. Suddenly, one of her paws shot down full length into the water and scooped up a crayfish, throwing it up on the shore. Of course, the baby coons knew what they were to do with it. This went on for several minutes and we noticed that she sometimes scooped up small perch and threw them ashore just as she did the crayfish. It would have been fun to continue watching all day long because tracks around the edge of the pond indicated almost all the animals of the forest came there to drink. We even saw deer tracks, but we already knew deer were in these woods. Who knows, we might even have seen that elusive panther if we had remained long enough.

We continued about another mile until we came to a large area of tall trees. The area almost seemed like virgin forest which had never been cut by the lumber people. Maybe it was virgin forest because it was a long way to a road and everyone knew that a virgin forest area did exist somewhere in the "deep woods." By this time the sun was about halfway to its zenith and it was about 9:30 according to Hubert's Ingersoll. Now it was time to hunt.

So with safety catches in the "safe" position we began creeping along like hunting Indians. Our eyes were focused on limbs high up in those huge trees.

Hubert said, "Even if we see a squirrel I don't believe our guns can bring him down as we have only number-six shot."

"Don't forget these shells we have are 'Super Express,' " I said. "Papa said this is all the power we need."

I didn't worry about the size of the shot because my gun was a full choke and had a longer barrel than Hubert's.

About two minutes after that whispered conversation, Hubert said, "Listen carefully, I hear a squirrel barking. Let's see if we can see him."

Sure enough, about seventy feet up a large oak, we saw a gray squirrel. We couldn't have noticed him against the gray of the limbs except that each time he barked, his long, curly tail jumped up and down.

"How do we get closer, close enough for a shot?" I asked.

That very second the squirrel moved around to the opposite side of the huge tree trunk. From there he could see us but we couldn't see him as his head was too small to see at that distance.

"I'll make my way around to the other side of the tree as quietly as possible. He will be keeping his eye on you. When I get to the other side I won't be able to see him but he will see me and move around to your side of the tree. Be ready, aim carefully, and bring him down," were Hubert's instructions.

So, Hubert began to circle the tree. I could see no movement at the spot where I thought the squirrel should be. When Hubert was directly opposite me on the far side of the huge oak he gently shook a small sapling about ten feet high. Sure enough, the squirrel scurried around to my side of the tree and I had a clear view of him. I aimed carefully, fired, and didn't know what happened for about a minute.

In my excitement, I had not rested the butt of my shotgun solidly against my shoulder. So when I fired, the butt of the kicking shotgun had hit me beside the head with a glancing blow. I dropped the gun and walked in circles for about half a minute. Hubert came running, wondering what had happened. He had seen the squirrel fall to the ground with a thump, but he didn't know the gun had kicked me almost into unconsciousness. After a couple of minutes my head cleared of its fogginess and I found that I had killed a large gray squirrel from long range. As a result, my head didn't hurt all that bad, especially each time I thought of the fat squirrel in my hunting knapsack.

We continued hunting in this fashion for about two hours and in our excitement forgot all about the sausage and biscuit sandwiches. In the meantime we bagged six squirrels, enough for a family supper with some left over. Once Hubert downed a squirrel running at full speed along a limb high up in a wild pecan tree.

Then he said, "We've got enough for one hunt. Let's sit down, rest, and eat by this small pond we crossed a few minutes ago."

So we sat down to eat and rest and talked about our good luck hunting. Suddenly, looking intently at me he said, "What in the world is the matter with your left cheek and eye?"

Not being able to see for myself with no mirror handy, I said, "What do you mean? Is something wrong?"

"It looks all bruised and is going to be black and blue before long," he replied.

Then it dawned upon both of us as to what had happened. When I fired at the squirrel the kick back of the gun butt coupled with the kick back to my hand had hit my cheek and eye so hard that I was temporarily addled and bruised. I didn't feel any real pain but was immediately bothered about what we would tell our dad who was always preaching about gun safety.

We talked that over, too, and decided there would be no way to hide my black eye and bruised cheek and we should just tell what happened. No doubt it had happened before. I had learned a good lesson: when firing any kind of gun always be sure the butt is resting soundly and solidly against the shoulder.

I said, "Now that we've got that settled let's go home and dress these squirrels. By the way, where is the sun? We were going to use it to guide us in getting home."

"I don't see any sun," Hubert said, "All I see is clouds."

While we were chasing squirrels, the sky had become gray with no sun to be seen anywhere.

To say we were startled is putting it mildly. We had counted on the sun. At 2:30 in the afternoon, we would know it was about one-third the distance necessary for the sun to move from its zenith to the point where it would set in the west. It would be slightly southwest of south and we would just turn in the opposite direction to get home—just slightly east of northeast. But where was the sun? Where was its zenith? We knew we should go north as a general direction, but which way was north? Entering the "deep woods," we had gone south; leaving the woods, we should go north. We had quite a bit of training in the woods, but we weren't prepared for the situation in which we found ourselves. Oh, for that little compass that we left home on the dresser. With it we could have followed the true northern course and known we were going in the right direction.

But farm boys who have spent lots of time hunting don't panic easily. We just stopped and talked it over.

I said, "Hubert, I have read that the bark on the north side of a tree is heavier and thicker to protect it from the cold, maybe we can use that method."

We examined several trees and couldn't see any difference in the bark. Then it dawned on me that the bark rule didn't apply very well as far south as Mississippi where the winters were not very severe. So we gave up that plan.

I always felt Hubert knew best in situations such as we were in and when he decided north was a certain direction, we set out to get out of those woods. No doubt about it, we were lost and at least four miles from the border of any cleared land. Just as we began, a thorny blackberry branch brushed my bruised cheek and scraped it so that the blood ran. I got angry at it and broke the vine into a 90° bend, in my anger thinking, "You won't hurt me again."

On and on we went, for about thirty minutes, during which time we had gone at least a mile. Then suddenly our surroundings looked familiar.

I said, "Hubert, we have been here before. Look, there is the blackberry vine I broke about half an hour ago."

It was then we realized we had done what so many persons lost in the woods had done before—walk in circles. I knew that people had actually died from exhaustion when lost in woods no more than one mile from safety.

Hubert said very matter of factly, "Well, let's face it, we are really lost and must come up with some plan to get us out of here. First, let's play a game. Let's each close his eyes and point in the direction he thinks north is supposed to be. Then when we open our eyes we will see if we agree."

We closed our eyes and pointed and when he said, "Now let's open our eyes," we discovered we were pointing in the same direction. We could call it fate or whatever, maybe our years of hunting in the woods, but we agreed and then I supplied the manner by which we could get out of the woods. If we were going in the right direction, at least we had a course of action, and that gave us a feeling of confidence. But deep within, each of us knew we didn't have a clue as to which direction was really north.

I had read in a scout manual or article of some kind dealing with scouts that two people can follow a straight line by sighting on a third object so that the two persons and the object are in line. Then the first person moves to the point of the object with the second carefully observing that he has walked straight. The person in the rear then selects an object far out in front of the first person and repeats the process over and over. This avoids the possibility of going in circles.

Many years later, as a squad leader in the army, I made use of this very system at night, having each member of the eight man squad advance only about ten yards, as one could only see about that far in the dark. In so doing, we moved in a straight line for seven miles through the woods.

After we had walked in a straight line for about forty-five minutes we stopped in discouragement, as we still had no proof we were going in the right direction.

Hubert said, "We just have to be going in the right direction. If not, they will get out search parties by dark and where will they look with the woods miles deep? Papa will know we had no compass and that it became cloudy, but he won't have any idea as to where we are. When night comes, if we aren't out, we can just make us a bed of leaves and wait until daylight. Then we can hear someone shooting a gun in alarm, or we can shoot ours to attract attention."

A gun could be heard about half a mile, we figured.

Our morale was getting pretty low at that time, but neither of us had any fear for our lives. We felt safe with each other. And then that much maligned and criticized railroad, the C. & G., came to our rescue. We knew it was to our north and that it had a 4:00 p.m. train that ran to Greenville. Its engineer never knew how sweet the sound of its steam whistle was, floating over a distance of more than three miles to us lost souls in the woods. We knew to go north to the railroad and we then knew we were headed in the right direction. I've always wondered if we would have lost confidence in our directions if that lonely whistle had not blown its beacon of hope. I'll never know the answer.

After the whistle sounded, we had renewed hope and boundless energy. We were out of the "deep woods" within forty-five minutes or so and heading across plowed fields long before dark. Before arriving, we knew we had to tell our parents something, but what should it be? If we told them how completely lost we were they would never let us hunt the "deep woods" again. So, for better or worse, we decided to make my bruised cheek and black eye the center of emphasis. When Papa asked me what happened I told him and he gave a short lecture on gun safety.

Then he asked, "With it becoming so cloudy and the compass at home, did you have any trouble with your direction?"

Hubert casually replied, "Oh, we got turned around once or twice, but we made it okay, and we sure did have fun watching a family of coons play around a pond."

The next night we had the best squirrel supper ever.

After hearing this story, Mark Williams, fourteen, our grandson, always thought we could have seen a deer if we had only looked carefully. Mark said he could not shoot a deer and wanted to write a poem about that feeling.

Only the Animals are Innocent

I was walking through the dew-kissed forest,
The sun had begun to rise.
It was like the woods were arranged by a florist,
Just for a lonely one's eyes.

"There goes a squirrel up an old oak tree."
I thought as the squirrel did so.
He was scurrying away from innocent me,
As if he thought me his foe.

My steps brought me to the edge of a a pond,
Tiny creatures began to flee.
It was their ground I was standing on,
But why run away from innocent me?

As I approached a large broken tree,
A noise came from behind my back.
I turned around and looked to see,
A harmless deer with a beautiful rack.

The handsome beast stood ever so still,
As he drank from the forest pool.
If I didn't try for this big kill,
Some would say I was a fool.

The deer looked horribly frightened,
As he shifted his gaze to me.
A finger on my right hand tightened,
It was on the trigger, you see.

My weapon may have caused some fear,
That day by the broken oak tree.
But I didn't end the life of the deer,
For he was the only innocent one of him and me.

By Mark Williams

Robbing a bee tree and chewing tobacco most certainly are quite different but much to my surprise they can be very closely related, as I found out when I was thirteen years old.

From the days of my earliest memory, my father chewed tobacco, and Brown Mule was his favorite. He didn't buy such small amounts as a plug or two at a time; he bought a box of it, a wooden, square box weighing about ten to fifteen pounds. He always wanted to be sure his supply of tobacco was adequate for him and any friend to whom he wanted to offer a chew.

His very favorite past time was to sit before the open fireplace after supper, read the *Commercial Appeal*, and chew and spit into the fireplace. The *Commercial Appeal*, next to tobacco, was his necessity. If the roads were impassable to the RFD deliveryman, someone usually walked the three miles to town and three miles back in order that Papa might have his newspaper. This became my lot about that time and my reward for walking the six miles was a cold, bubbly root beer that cost five cents. I felt the reward was fair, but would have gone if ordered to do so anyway.

As Papa read his newspaper, we kids of school age would gather around two small tables, each bearing a kerosene lamp, to study the next day's assignments in school. There were always four or five of us at home studying each night around the tables. The lamps didn't give off much light, but Papa always said that if Abraham Lincoln could study to become a lawyer by candlelight, we could surely study by kerosene lamps which Abe Lincoln would have been glad to have had. The scene—Papa reading his newspaper, the kids studying, Mother sewing by hand or reading some kind of journal—was an absolutely quiet one. There was no conversation except when one kid would ask an older one to help with some question at hand. Any such question would be in a whisper.

The only noise came about when Papa would lower his newspaper and spit into the open fire. When the tobacco juice met the flame or hot coals there would be a sizzling noise and steam would momentarily rise from the burning fire. Papa wasn't very accurate with his spitting. He had hit the wood facing around the fireplace and the board just above the fireplace, which held up the mantel, so many times that they were a mottled brown color. No doubt Mother abhorred this. She tried many times to wash the tobacco stain off the wood, but it just wouldn't come clean. Still, it would have been completely out of character for Mother to have said anything aloud about Papa's spitting. I don't know if it were out of fear or love; maybe a bit of both.

One night there were two extra characters to the scene described above. Mr. Johnson, about 300 pounds, with a very round cherubic face, had come over to talk farming with Papa. Mr. Johnson was an important man. He managed a whole section of land which adjoined our quarter section. Mr. Johnson also chewed tobacco and was no more accurate when spitting in the fireplace than Papa. They were busily talking farming and politics as we kids studied as usual.

The other character was my oldest sister, who was visiting home on a short vacation from business school in Jackson. Clara was the only one who had been in a city for any lengthy period of time and we kids looked up to her and thought she was pretty much on top of everything. She always seemed to have a mind of her own. She could express herself well and could disagree with Papa better than any of the other kids. She was open and straight-forward with what she said to our parents and didn't beat around the bush in talking to them.

I have often thought Clara was bored that particular night that Mr. Johnson was visiting. On the other hand, she may have only had a headache, but whatever the cause, she wasn't in a happy mood.

After a half dozen or so spits, with both Mr. Johnson and Papa missing part of the time, Clara suddenly burst out with the following, "Papa, that chewing and spitting into the fire is the dirtiest, filthiest habit I have ever seen. Just look what you have done to the wood around the fireplace. I think you could at least get closer to the fire and not stain the woodwork."

It may be she said some other things, but we kids were in a state of shock and I can't be sure of what else she said. Who could have imagined Sister would speak to Papa like that, especially with Mr. Johnson present.

After a moment or two of silence, Mr. Johnson said, "Well, Gilbert, I guess I should be heading home."

He got up and left with Papa seeing him to the door. Then Papa returned to his rocking chair, raised his paper to continue reading, and moved closer to the fireplace so as to be more accurate with his spitting. Clara, after her outburst, left the room, and probably cried in privacy. Of course, none of us kids said a word. We just continued studying. We knew that was no time for idle talk or comment.

The next day, I think about noon, Papa came in from the fields and in a voice all could hear, said, " Well, I've been chewing tobacco about thirty years but I have had my last chew."

He then placed a half a plug of Brown Mule tobacco on the plank that surrounded the front porch just under the overhanging roof. We kids kept close watch on the partially chewed plug of tobacco. In fact, we watched it until it dried and curled up in wafer-like leaves from which it had been made. This must have been for two or more years and Papa never chewed it again.

About this time in our lives, Papa got the reputation of being the best bee-tree robber there was in the area. Few people had tame, domestic-type bee hives because they could get plenty of honey by robbing bee trees.

Many of the large oak, elm, or pecan trees that grew in the woods around our farm and along the bayou shores had hollow places in them. Squirrels used these areas for warm winter nests if bees didn't beat them to it. Bees would find one of those hollow trees, sometimes even more than one swarm, clean out all the decayed material and then start making and storing honey in the hollow area. They were busiest in the spring when flowers and alfalfa were in bloom. We never robbed bee trees of their honey after July, because we knew they would have to find a new location for their home and still have time enough to generate a supply for their own food during the winter.

Around July 25 my father got an invitation to lead a crew in robbing a number of bee trees along a bayou a few miles west of our home town near Indianola, the county seat. The trees had already been selected by the land owner. It was about two months after Papa quit chewing tobacco, and the huge flood had receded.

Following the usual procedure, we cut the first tree down with cross cut saws. My father had a number of smoking faggots already burning. Just as the tree fell with a loud bang he rushed in with his smoking faggots and laid them on the ground directly below the hole the bees used to go into and out of the hollow tree. Smoke seems to addle mad bees and take the fight out of them, but it doesn't kill them. A few angry bees had stung my father before the smoke began to take effect, but this was nothing new. He had always allowed bees to sting him in small numbers. As the smoke took effect we moved in with saws and wedges and split out a section of the trunk of the tree. Revealed in the open space was a large amount of beautiful honeycomb already filled with honey. All Papa had to do was break it out in large chunks and place the chunks of honeycomb in a zinc wash tub placed near where he was working. This tree and its one hive of bees contained a large tub of honey.

We moved from tree to tree, taking about thirty minutes to extract the honey from each tree. A crew would be busy cutting down one tree while Papa was removing the honey from another. Each time a few bees stung him before they became listless from the smoke screen he always had available. After robbing a few trees he began to tell us that the bee stings were hurting him for the first time in many years.

As we cut down the fifth tree, Papa said he believed he would use a net over his head, neck, and shoulders to prevent the bees from getting directly to him. At the time he had already placed the smoking faggot under the bee hole. Suddenly one of the smoking faggots flamed up unexpectedly and set the net on fire. Papa began pulling and tugging at the burning net, but he couldn't seem to get it off his head. So he did the next best thing possible. He ran about five steps and dived head first into the shallow, stagnant water of the bayou. As he went under, of course the flame went out and a small cloud of steam hovered over the spot where he had dived in. Within a few seconds he had freed his head and shoulders from the muddy bottom of the bayou and stood up. Papa was embarrassed by the whole episode, which seemed very funny after we found that he had only been singed by the flames. We complimented him upon his diving form and imitated the manner in which he tried to tear the net off his head. Louis, eleven at the time, suggested to Papa that he try out for the Olympic diving team. This didn't seem so funny to Papa and we soon found out why.

A few minutes later the entire picture changed. Papa said he hurt terribly and we noted his face and neck were badly swollen.

He said, "Boys, I just can't rob any more trees today. I can hardly stand up."

He sat down and for the first time in my life I heard my father groan from pain. We knew something serious was making him very sick. My uncle had brought his T-Model pick-up, and said he thought Papa should be taken to a doctor. Indianola was only four miles away and the town had a hospital. We loaded Papa in the seat but he could hardly sit up. Uncle Earl sped as fast as he could over the rough gravel roads to the hospital. Louis and I rode in the truck bed.

There was a doctor on duty when we came roaring up to the rear entrance to the hospital. He quickly asked what Papa had been doing after he saw how swollen his face, neck, and arms were.

Uncle Earl said, "Robbing bee trees, and he's been stung quite a lot."

The doctor knew exactly what to do: there was an anti-toxin in all hospitals and doctors' offices in the area for sting and snake-bite victims. He quickly put Papa to bed after giving him a shot of pain killer and another shot for bee sting. Papa seemed to get worse and worse, and his breathing more and more difficult. The doctor said we would just have to hope the anti-toxin took effect quickly.

After about an hour we knew Papa was better when he said, " Well boys, I think I'm going to make it. I feel better already."

The doctor told us we had just as well go home, since Papa would have to spend the night in the hospital for observation. He walked outside and asked us if Papa had always let bees sting him, almost at will. When we told him, "Yes", he asked us if by chance Papa chewed tobacco.

We said, "Yes, but he quit about a month and a half ago."

"That explains it," he said. "The nicotine and other ingredients in the tobacco were their own anti-toxin protecting him from the bee sting poison. But during the last month this has gotten out of his system and the poison affects him just as it does anyone else. So, he must never rob bee trees again while letting bees sting him."

When we told him abut the net catching on fire he said, "Well I thought I could tell that his hair and eyebrows were singed, but I didn't figure bee stings had done that."

When we got back to the scene of the tree robbing, the crew was sitting around talking and wondering what had happened. We reported that Papa would have to stay in the hospital overnight but that his bee tree robbing days were over unless he wore a net. Then we all loaded the truck with the honey and our tools and took off for home. Although nobody said so, I knew everyone was relieved things turned out no worse than they did. I also knew for the first time that there was a connection between chewing tobacco and robbing bee trees. With Papa on the mend, I began to think how good that honey would taste on hot buttered biscuits when winter came.

Now-a-days most parents think their kids should have their own private bedrooms, and I guess that's a pretty good thing. They put up their own pictures, mostly of rock stars or movie actors, or pennants or slogans of one kind or another. Having one's own room gives one a chance to be alone to daydream or listen to music or sleep. One can tell by entering any teenager's room whether the occupant is a boy or girl without even looking in the closet at the clothes. They usually have their own TV or stereo and any number of radios and electric clocks. Well, that's not like my room was when I was that age.

By the time I was a teenager I had my own room, but until that time there were so many kids in the house that three of us boys slept in one long room that was much like a dormitory and there was no privacy. Truthfully, we didn't need any privacy because our rooms were only for dressing or sleeping as we were usually dead tired by the time we got into them at night. During the school year we studied around tables in the living room with kerosene lamps furnishing the light, and after study it was straight to bed. In summer, after working in the fields, we took baths in washtubs half-full of water, which had been set out in the sun to warm up during the afternoon. After those baths we hit the sack and were asleep within minutes. There was no music, stereo, or TV. Television hadn't even been invented and neither had electric clocks or stereos. But in the first place, we had no electricity, therefore not even an electric refrigerator.

I can see my room today just as it was then. Bare planks on the walls with no pictures. Bare planks on the ceiling with no covering, and bare planks for floors except that my floor had a couple of tanned deer hides for rugs. When kids came into my room and saw the deer hides they always wanted to know where the deer had been shot. To answer them I had to turn the hide over with fur down and then they could see three neat holes where the buckshot had entered the deer's body. The other hide had several holes in it and I guess it was shot when close-up to the hunter. So there was nothing in my room that was entertaining. For a time we had a gramophone with a spring handle, on which we played records after winding it up. As the years passed the spring got weaker and weaker and then, finally, it broke. To my recollection, it was never repaired. But I had a secret place to which I would go when I was lonely or felt I wanted to be alone. Mother knew about it and seemed to understand. Nothing was ever said about it to the other kids.

On lonesome Sunday afternoons, or perhaps Saturday when I had no one to visit and no trip planned to town, I would quietly head for the woods only a quarter mile away. These particular woods were called "the pasture" for want of a better name, but it is true we grazed the cows and mules there at times. Really, it was only about fifteen acres and the trees had been allowed to grow there for perhaps sixty years. Some of the oaks were eighty or ninety feet high and were gnarled and twisted. They had been passed over by the loggers when the whole country was cut over many years before because they would not produce good lumber. And then there was the cypress tree, right in the middle of the small forest. This cypress was said to be over 1500 years old. It was about 150 feet high, towering over everything around it. Hawks and owls perched in its upper branches and could see everything that went on for miles around and know they were safe from marauders. This tree was about six feet in diameter and it was perhaps fifty feet up the trunk to the first limb. Lightning had hit it many times during thunderstorms but the results of the lightning bolts were only scars down the entire trunk. No matter how strong the bolt of lightning might be, the trunk shook its effects off and survived.

Cypress trees need lots of water and this one grew by a stagnant pool that was no more than two feet deep and fifty yards across. This pool was the only one that had water in it in the heat of summer, so you can imagine that it was the gathering place for all the wild life that lived in the woods. Squirrels, rabbits, owls, hawks, raccoons and possums came there to drink in late afternoon when the sun was casting long shadows, giving them a sense of security. I was their unexpected visitor but they seldom saw me unless I wanted them to.

When growing up, I learned to move through the woods almost as quietly as an Indian while hunting with Hubert. He was six feet tall by the time he was fifteen but he could move so quietly even in dry leaves that one wouldn't hear him. When hunting squirrels we whispered to each other so as not to be heard. This training helped me when I wanted to be alone on those quiet, hot, summer evenings. Perhaps fifty years before, a cypress tree had fallen and it extended from a point about twenty-five feet from the pond to a point near the middle of the pond. A hackberry tree had grown up alongside the fallen cypress and it was there that I went to be alone. With my back propped against the hackberry and my feet extended along the cypress log I could be very comfortable and not need to move for hours at a time. Here, I could commune with nature, if it can be described that way. I always dressed in something dark, never wearing a white shirt. You see, I learned about camouflage before it became so well known in World War II.

I got there before sundown, got comfortably arranged with my back to the hackberry, and began my wait. I didn't wait long until I had company. First, a squirrel came down the body of the huge cypress in his little fits and starts, headfirst, carefully surveying his surroundings to see if danger lurked. Life in the forest is pretty much a case of survival of the fittest and all animals and birds seem to be constantly alert as many animals prey on others. Hawks eat birds and mice and so do owls. Snakes swallow fish and even small rabbits. It happens all the time as I saw for myself.

One Sunday afternoon small bits and pieces of some kind of berries began to fall on my head. Perhaps a half inch at a time I began elevating my head to see where the debris was coming from. There, about twenty feet above me, a squirrel was nibbling hackberries. The leftovers were falling on my shoulders and head. After a few minutes, I guess Mr. Squirrel got thirsty and started down the trunk of the hackberry against which I was leaning. I could hear his claws grasping the rough bark as he made his way down. I got stone still then, and slowly closed my eyes until they were about one-fourth open. This enabled me to see but not blink. I had found that if a squirrel so much as sees a person blink he knows it's the enemy and heads for a hole in a tree while barking as loudly as he can to warn everything within hearing distance.

But this time I fooled him into thinking I was just another friendly object in the forest. He gently put his front paws on my shoulder. I thought he would see the vein in my neck throbbing with excitement but he didn't. He then ran gently down my shirtfront and along my legs before running out the length of the log to the water. What a thrill it was to fool such a wary animal!

Time passed. The squirrel jumped off the log at the edge of the pond and at about the same time action picked up. A huge owl with noisy wings landed on the log and took his drink a few drops at a time. Then a white heron about three feet tall glided down through the tree limbs which made a canopy over the pond. Before dark came a mother coon and her brood of four furry little coons. She played with them as they drank from the pond. She did some fishing there too, slapping at large minnows and flopping them onto the bank.

By the time darkness came I had seen almost every species of bird and animal living in those woods and was so stiff from sitting motionless that I had to move. My movement put an end to animal and bird watching. Squirrels I hadn't seen began barking, but the biggest racket of all was raised by the birds. Birds seem to be the watchdogs of the forest. They not only warn others of their greatest enemy, the hawks, but they also make a chorus of sound when humans invade their territory.

It was by this pond and on that cypress log that I spent many late summer afternoons in my favorite place to be alone. It didn't necessarily mean that I was lonely, but I guess I really was. But how do I really know? All I could be sure of was that I felt more at peace with myself and my surroundings when I arose to walk the short distance home in the darkening shadows.

The following poem was written by my grandson, Mark Williams, after hearing this story. His poem might not win any awards for poetic form, but the thought it presents is deeper than normal for a fourteen year old.

Loneliness Can Be Aloneness But the Two are Not the Same

Aloneness is when you're without any others,
And think totally for yourself.
Maybe you like to be alone,
Uninterrupted by someone else.

Loneliness is when you feel empty inside,
Thinking no one's there for you.
Maybe you wish you weren't alone,
This is when loneliness is aloneness, too.

Loneliness is not always being alone,
Being alone is not always loneliness.
If someone is with you but doesn't care,
You're not alone, but without happiness.

If being alone is something you like
You don't have to be lonely, too.
You can think for yourself and get things done,
Sometimes the one you need is you.

Mark Williams

Chapter 9

FIRST LOVES

Did other boys or girls get crushes on their teachers? How was I to know, when nobody ever talked about their teachers when they had special feelings for them? I certainly wasn't about to discuss the way I felt about Miss Broadhood.

Miss Broadhood was my sixth grade teacher. She was not only the best teacher I ever had in grade school, but she was also the prettiest. If I had owned an apple orchard she would have had a big apple from me every day. All of her kids had good feelings about her, but maybe not in the same way I did. I can't say for sure about the others, as kids have a way of keeping their secret feelings to themselves just as adults do. Even when she walked up the aisle and her dress brushed my desk, I got a thrill out of her presence. And it might be the cologne she wore had something to do with that, too. Each day I went eagerly to school, looking forward to the first glimpse of the day of her.

One day I noticed Franklin Spencer hanging around her desk after school. He wanted to know if he could dust the erasers which we used to erase chalk marks on the blackboard. Blackboards were big in those days, usually covering two sides of a classroom. Students were called upon to go to the blackboard very often to demonstrate how to write a sentence or do a math problem.

Hearing Franklin ask if he could help her was good grounds for jealousy right then and there, because she always let me wash the blackboard with a damp cloth, and empty waste baskets. But Franklin was the one person I couldn't be jealous of. He had been my friend from the first grade and this friendship lasted through junior college. His parents treated me almost as if I were a son. Franklin and I were almost always rivals for any scholastic honors available, but there was just no way we could be serious rivals for Miss Broadhood's affection, because, as it turned out, she had enough affection for both of us.

Near the end of the school term, Miss Broadhood announced she would not be back to teach in Moorhead the next year. She planned to teach nearer her home in the hills of east Mississippi. One can't imagine how much this upset me. Even to have her teaching in the same building was okay, but to have her gone forever just seemed too much to bear.

Because of the way I felt about her and because of seeing that Franklin had a special feeling for her, one day I asked Franklin how he felt about her leaving. I found that he was just as sad and upset about it as I was. Because of this mutual feeling, Franklin and I became even closer. Still, I just couldn't believe anyone could love her as much as I did.

Because of our trust in each other, Franklin and I discussed her clothes and how pretty she looked at times, but these conversations were when there was no one else around.

One day I said, "Franklin, I just can't have her leave without kissing her goodbye, but I just don't know how I could ever get up nerve to kiss her. Do you think you could?"

"Not unless both of us take a solemn oath that we will kiss her on the last day of school," he replied.

The end of school neared and as often as we could, Franklin and I walked by the huge Lucas home where she roomed and boarded, in hopes of seeing her. Quite often she would be sitting in the front porch swing. Almost every nice house had a front porch swing. No homes were air conditioned and quite often, on a hot day, the swing was a refuge from the heat. During the last week of school she often invited us to come sit in the shade on the porch with her. Of course, we were very happy to do this. We always talked about how the end of school was approaching. She tried to reassure us that we would have a very fine teacher next year and would forget all about her. We knew we might have a good teacher, but certainly not one about whom we felt as we did her.

We began to plan how to go about kissing Miss Broadhood on the last day of school. There was some safety and support in there being two of us. Alone, neither could have made such serious plans as the one we came up with. We would just finish doing the chores we did for her and then we would just walk up to her desk where we assumed she would be sitting and each would kiss her soundly on the cheek. We also assumed there would be no one else around at the time.

Finally, the last day of school arrived. The final bell of the day rang and kids collected their belongings and headed home. Franklin and I didn't.

He asked, "Miss Broadhood, it wouldn't be right to leave all the trash in the waste baskets and the blackboard all marked up, would it?"

She replied, "Of course not, would you boys help me as you usually do?"

The truth was we were sparring for time and trying to build up nerve to do what we had planned, but if Franklin felt as I did, this was to be to no avail. I just knew I couldn't follow through on my oath, but I couldn't tell Franklin this.

After what seemed an eternity in time, she said, "Well, boys, that's about it. Things are ready for the janitor and I must go home and pack up as I take the train tomorrow to go home. But first I have a surprise for you. Would you come up here to my desk?"

Of course, we went. Wild horses couldn't have held us twelve-year-olds back.

When I came near her she suddenly hugged me, a real body hug, not one where people hug each other by each leaning over about a foot to go through the motions of a hug. Her hug was real, it was firm, and it was warm. Then she kissed me solidly on the cheek. I really didn't get to kiss her, but what did it matter? She had hugged and kissed me and I didn't have to chicken out. She then did the same for Franklin. We then turned, told her goodbye, and left the room. We were speechless.

On the way home, we were silent with excitement for quite a time and then we began to talk about our good luck.

"Wilson," Franklin said, "Miss Broadhood kept me from being a coward. I could never have done what we planned."

Then I told him the same thing could be applied to me, that I just didn't have the nerve at the last minute.

That summer, the two of us talked many times about one of the biggest and most exciting secrets of our twelve-year-old lives. We had a good teacher the next year, but there would never be another Miss Broadhood.

During that next summer, while working on our farm, I spent lots of time daydreaming about what a beautiful person Miss Broadhood was, and how thrilling the goodbye kiss was that she gave me. But this was a teacher-pupil relationship, and quite different from my feelings for Laurie Bell, who was a classmate.

Laurie rode the school bus from the little town of Sunflower, about ten miles north of Moorhead. In those days grade school was from the first through the eighth grade. I rode a different school bus from our farm home three miles south of town.

Laurie and I had been in the same class from the first grade. All that time I thought of Laurie as just another pesky blond girl with knobby knees. In the fifth and sixth grade we were strong rivals in arithmetic and the two of us were the best in the class. Both of us made good grades in all our subjects but it was in arithmetic that we clashed for top honors.

Each year all of the schools in our county had what was known as a literary meet—just like a track meet—only this was for classroom subjects and was to determine who was first, second, or third in our county in each subject in each grade. It was a big thing for our school, and as a school we always hoped to come out with more points than any other.

Our teacher had a hard time trying to decide whether Laurie or I should represent our school in seventh grade arithmetic. She decided to pick the class representative by having a contest on the blackboard in front of the whole class. No doubt this made Laurie as nervous as I was but neither of us would have admitted it because of pride. Usually, I could do arithmetic faster than Laurie and this always made her mad, but I didn't know if she had caught on to my secret of how to beat her. I knew if she had, I could lose and would have to represent my class in spelling instead of arithmetic.

We were sent out of the room and when in the hall outside the classroom door we didn't speak to each other. I guess it was because we were such strong rivals and didn't want to admit any weakness to the other. As we stood outside, our teacher put a whole blackboard full of arithmetic on the board. This included four digit adding, four digit multiplication, and subtraction and division as well. She then covered the blackboard with paper and called us in. The subtraction and division were to be done first with multiplication and adding last.

When she said, "Go," we started.

Later, Franklin Spencer told me that Laurie was ahead of me when the subtraction and division were finished. I caught up with her on the multiplication, but didn't know it at the time as I didn't dare take my eyes off what I was doing. When I finished the arithmetic I quickly dropped my crayon on the rack below the board. Laurie dropped hers about five seconds later and I had beaten her again. She got mad at me as usual, but she got to represent our grade in another subject.

I guess I felt sorry for her, and at recess told her my secret for adding and subtracting which saved time. I told her that when adding long columns of figures the amount that was to be carried over to the next column should be carried in your memory and added to the next column rather than using the old method of writing the carry-over number at the top of the next column. The same rule applied to multiplication. The little time it takes to make a written notation of the number adds up to quite a bit of time when adding long four digit columns.

Laurie said, "Well, I'll be darned, I never thought of that, but doesn't it take lots of practice?"

I said, "Sure it takes practice, but it sure saves time."

Those were the first serious words we ever spoke to each other. Most of our other spoken words were in anger, or to make fun of the other, or something normal for boys and girls to say when they were teasing.

Something prevailed upon me to take a second look at Laurie. Everybody liked her. She was the tallest girl in class, about half a head taller than I in the seventh grade. Suddenly, her long, blond, curly hair was pretty. Her eyes were blue and her complexion was like peaches and cream. It had just struck me; Laurie Bell was a pretty girl and her knees weren't knobby anymore. From that time on, I didn't make off-hand remarks just to make her mad or make fun of her. Still, she was taller than I and so I just admired her from a distance, all the while pretending I didn't notice her as being special.

Laurie was into girls track and basketball which were popular sports at the time. She was just an all-around outstanding girl and there was no getting away from that.

Laurie didn't seem to have any favorite boys and none that I knew of claimed her as his girl friend. One day I wrote her a note when we were in the ninth grade, the first grade of high school. We had a clever way of folding notes into a very small package so they wouldn't come unfolded. Note writing and reading were very secretive and always required a go-between as a deliveryman. But their delivery was about as dependable as the U.S. mail. The delivery person was honor bound not to unfold and read the notes. Secrets were honored by all.

My first note to Laurie was to ask her if she would save a place for me at the table where we ate our sack lunches. She did not answer at all that day and neither did she say a word about having gotten my note. Why are girls like that, I wondered? After that I decided it was just a girl's way of not letting a boy know where he stands with her or how she feels about him. I thought Laurie might be just taking her time to look me over and thinking about whether she wanted my name to be connected to hers in the ways boys and girls did, such as Laurie plus Wilson or L.B. plus W.F.

Surprise! Surprise! The next day she saved a place for me to sit by her. Of course, nothing was said about it. She couldn't have admitted she saved a place for me at that time. Maybe she would later, but not then. We were still at sparring distance the first day. There was no privacy around the lunch table, but that was a good thing because I wouldn't have known what to do about privacy at that point. I would have been scared to death about being alone with her right then.

In all the years I had known Laurie we had not so much as brushed hands, but now we began writing notes on a daily basis. For a while she signed them, "Your friend". Hers were delivered to me at the end of the school day and I stuffed them deep into my pockets. Of course, I read them when I got off the school bus. But then I read them again by kerosene lamp light after I got in bed at night. The next morning I stuffed her notes into the back end of my dresser drawer. I never knew what she did with mine. Just about that time she began signing her notes, "Luv, Laurie," (nobody our age would have used the word "Love" as that word had too much meaning).

Each noon hour all the kids who came by bus ate in the game room and then played games—that is, when the weather was bad outside. There was lots of noise and some pranks pulled even with a teacher on duty.

The game room was just off the auditorium where we had chapel each day. All classes sat in their own areas for chapel. By this time, Laurie and I saved seats for the other so we could sit together. This was a happy part of the day. The truth is I wanted others to think Laurie was my girl, although I wasn't a bit sure she was. Still, a little thing like saving a seat was one good sign.

Chapel was a short religious service which began with a couple of hymns. This was followed by a short devotional period after which a prayer dismissed us to go back to class. Mr. Vandiver, the superintendent, always read a few verses from the Bible during the chapel service. His favorite song was "In the Garden", with "Onward Christian Soldiers" running a close second. His favorite saying was "Pretty is as pretty does." I was not sure what that meant except that it had something to do with conduct.

The big trouble wasn't planned. It just happened like trouble often does. The piano used to accompany our songs was an old-style upright type. One day after finishing lunch we were playing around aimlessly when I reached inside the piano and plucked some of the strings on the sounding board. As expected, when I pulled on several of them they gave off different tones. Where the thought came from I don't know, but I asked some of the kids what would happen if we put paper wads under the strings so they couldn't vibrate. Nobody knew but we tried the idea, and of course, no sound was forthcoming when we plucked that string or struck the key connected to the string. On a dare from someone, I stuffed paper wads under five or six of the strings. Then the trick was to wait until we had chapel the next day to see what would happen.

Chapel started the next day on schedule with Mr. Vandiver reading from the Bible.

Suddenly he pointed to me and said, "Wilson, recite one verse from the Bible."

I froze, thinking someone had tattled, and he had picked me out to recite the verse as punishment. As it turned out, he didn't know about the paper wads at that time.

After about a minute after getting over my sudden fright I said, "God is Love."

"Fine," he said, "That is one of the Bible's most meaningful verses."

Then he went on with his speech to which we paid little attention. Laurie was sitting by me when Mr. Vandiver called on me. Because I froze for a moment and was speechless, she must have thought I was asleep because she punched me in the ribs with her elbow and then acted as if she hadn't done it.

After the short devotional talk, Mr. Vandiver said, "Now, we will sing two hymns."

I don't remember their names for good reason, as I was shaking in my shoes, wondering what would happen when the teacher played the piano. The music teacher went to the piano, opened her hymn book, and began to play. Everything sounded just fine for a moment. When we were almost through the first line of the song, suddenly the piano gave off a 'thoink' kind of sound. Then after a moment a different key gave off nothing but silence. Then another and another. Finally, she gave up in wonderment as to what was wrong with the usually trustworthy piano.

Mr. Vandiver stopped singing and went over to examine the piano and to try to find the trouble. A faint snicker spread across the student body. No doubt the word had spread to everyone by this time. Finally, Mr. Vandiver located the paper wads and pulled them out one at a time for all to see. Then there was mild laughter throughout the student body. Laurie looked down, put her hands over her face and avoided laughing out loud. After the removal of the paper wads the songs were sung with all the keys on the piano working perfectly.

At the conclusion of the songs, Mr. Vandiver lowered his glasses on his nose and stared at the entire group of students; but of course, I felt he was staring at me alone. I expected him to say, "All right, I want the ones who put paper wads in the piano to stand up." What would I have done if he had? Would I have stood up and confessed although I was only one of three involved? I'll never know because he only went on with his announcements of the day and didn't say a word about the piano. But saying anything was not necessary as his stare said it all, "If this happens again someone will have to answer for it."

I wasn't very big on playing pranks, it just wasn't my nature; but a few days after the piano incident I pulled one that put an end to a beautiful boy-girl relationship. As I explained earlier, after eating lunch in the game room, we milled around in the auditorium where we had chapel service. There was a balcony above the stage of the auditorium and on this particular day some of the boy-girl duos went up there for some togetherness where all could not see us. Some of us got our first kisses, boy-girl type, over that auditorium and it was there that I kissed Laurie for the last time. Our kisses were very brief and unemotional—just plain kisses with little if any embracing and having no lasting meaning. But they were kisses just the same and so important to us. At least they were to me, because Laurie was now so pretty with her beautiful long tresses and her fair skin. I truly cared for her, as a ninth grader can, and considered her my girl.

But I put a stop to a cherished friendship without knowing it was going to happen. To this day I am embarrassed to tell what I did, but it was really very innocently done.

After one of those boy-girl get-togethers, a week or so after the piano incident, the girls went down to the main floor of the auditorium which was under the front of the balcony. One of the boys noticed a dead mouse lying against a wall. He picked it up by the tail and handed it to me. Then an impish thought got the best of me. Why not drop it down on the group of girls who were gathered just below and in front of the balcony? I expected to drop the mouse and hear the girls scream in fright and all would quiet down, but luck was against me that day.

Honestly, I didn't aim at Laurie, but that mouse dropped down the back of her neck underneath her blouse that had an open collar. At first she didn't know what happened and didn't know what the object was until one of the girls helped her get the mouse out. When she saw the mouse she keeled over in a dead faint—what girl wouldn't have, I've often asked myself.

That thoughtless, but unplanned prank marked the end of our sweet relationship. Laurie never forgot it nor forgave me. At least that's the way it seemed. There were no more notes, no friendly smiles, no efforts to save a place for me to sit beside her at lunch or in chapel. Yet, on the last day of school when she walked out of the building to the school bus, I was only a few feet behind her. As she mounted the first step of the bus, she turned and looked back. Of course, she saw me on the sidewalk and just for an instant, a tiny, tiny instant, I saw her faint smile directed my way and a small wave of her hand which she had freed from holding her books. Was I forgiven? I've always hoped so.

Chapter 10

"THE MIGHTY MUDDY"

Anyone who has seen the Mississippi River close up knows why the Indians called it the "Father of Waters". No other river in the United States even approaches it in size and in the volume of water it carries. I knew this from things I had studied in school.

We had lived in Mississippi for eight years, from the time I was three until I was eleven, and yet I had not seen the Mississippi River, which was only 35 miles away. Just think: only 35 miles! Naturally, I wanted to see it, so I was really excited when my Uncle Earl, who had a Model-T touring car at the time, suggested he take our family on an all-day outing to see the Mississippi. It was a real adventure to actually see the river which was to wreak such havoc on the Delta Country two years later. What a river it must be, I thought. The history books said its flooding had built up all the land in the Delta, even our farm, over thousands of years when there were no levees to hold it back in the wet season and when the snow melting up north caused it to flood.

Mother planned a picnic lunch for all of us and on the appointed day, we loaded into Uncle Earl's car and set out. For the first twenty miles the roads were very rough, as they were built of gravel and not graded very often. It was a hot, dry day and the dust was almost strangling, but that didn't bother me because I was so excited about the trip that I hardly noticed it. Mother tried to avoid some of it by keeping a handkerchief over her nose and mouth for most of the trip.

When we were about 25 miles from home, near Leland, Uncle Earl said he wanted to make a side trip a few miles south to see an Indian mound in which he had taken an interest. His interest, I found when we got to the mound, came about because a new road was being built on a right-of-way that cut through the Indian mound. What the tractors uncovered was what Uncle Earl wanted to see. He was interested in Indian lore and wanted to see what arrowheads, clay pots, or even Indian skeletons were uncovered by the tractors and graders. He had some Indian bones at home in a cabinet, he said.

I never could figure out why the Indians wanted to live in the flat Delta country in the first place. I guess it was because of so much wild game being there. They were subjected to flooding and no doubt they got malaria just as we did. These huge mounds were built by millions of baskets of dirt the Indians dug nearby and carried by hand. When Indians died they were not buried in holes. Instead, they were buried on top of the ground and then covered with dirt. Each death caused the mound to grow just a little bit. The mound the road was cutting through was one of the largest, about 35 feet high and 200 feet across. It would provide safety for lots of Indians from the flood water and a burial ground for many also. Later, these mounds provided sites for some beautiful homes. There is one ten miles south of Leland now.

When we arrived at the mound, huge amounts of dirt had been removed that day. I surely didn't like what I saw. There were Indians bones scattered everywhere. Also, there were arrowheads, broken pieces of pottery, and other Indian artifacts scattered about. To me it seemed cruel and thoughtless to tear down an Indian mound in order to build a road. They could have run the road around the mound. I wondered what we would have thought if someone planned to run a road through the Moorhead cemetery. The truth is no one would have done such a thing.

After looking at what was going on we collected a few arrowheads and broken pieces of pottery and then continued our trip. No one kept any of the Indian bones as souvenirs and I surely was glad of that.

When back on the main road to Greenville, a city that was built right beside the river, the dust was as bad as ever. And to make matters worse, we got behind another car that was kicking up lots of dust. We "ate" the lead car's dust for miles. Uncle Earl buzzed his horn many times to no avail. The horns just made a buzzing sound when a button on the front door was pushed. It didn't even make an "ooga-ooga-ooga" sound as later horns made. Roads were rough and cars were noisy. There were no rear view mirrors and so the man driving the car in front didn't even know we were following him. If he had, most likely he would have slowed down, pulled over and almost stopped in order to let us pass safely on the narrow road.

Finally Uncle Earl said, "I'm going to put a stop to this and I know just exactly what to do."

He reached under his front seat and pulled out a Colt .45 automatic pistol he had brought home from World War I. He aimed at the ditch on the left side of the road and pulled the trigger. It made a monstrous blast about like a shotgun or half a stick of dynamite.

The driver in front pulled over to the side of the road and stopped. He got out and inspected his tires to see if one had blown out. As we passed, he looked quizzically at us and I'm sure, must have wondered what had caused such a huge blast. In those days tires had sixty to seventy pounds of pressure per square inch, and when one blew out it could be heard for long distances. So it was natural that with no blown tire the driver must have been puzzled.

When we reached Leland, only ten miles from our destination, we got a chance to drive on the first concrete paved road in the Delta—some people said it was the first concrete road in the state. The strip of concrete was about ten feet wide, plenty wide for a car to drive on it, but when a car met another each had to slow down and allow the outside wheels to run on the gravel shoulder. We kids were really impressed, as the concrete was ten miles long running all the way from Greenville to Leland. It ran through the town of Greenville and up and over the levee of the Mississippi River.

The nearer the river we got, the more excited we were. Uncle Earl found his way through town, slowed down, and finally stopped at the point where the road led up to the levee. He wanted to have a look before driving up to the top of it. We sat anxiously waiting for him to return.

When he got back, he cranked the car and started up the paving to the top of the levee without hesitation. When we reached the top we could hardly believe what we were seeing; a huge river, brown in color due to silt, and almost a mile wide.

Greenville was almost like a seaport. Barges and steamboats with passengers were tied up to the wharf made of brick paving. The wharf was about 250 yards long and reached from the top of the levee down into the water, but I don't know how far. It must have been built sometime when the river was very low because it reached down into the water the day we saw it.

Uncle Earl made a slow turn about halfway down the wharf and then stopped parallel with the river. As we stopped and were looking around, some driver who must have had more nerve than brains drove down to the water and then along its edge, with two of the wheels on the river's side splashing along in the water. I couldn't help wondering what would have happened if he had lost control and his front wheels suddenly turned into deeper water. Maybe he could have jumped and swum out, as it was a touring car and not an enclosed sedan. I was glad Uncle Earl didn't want to wash his car wheels off that way.

This was a historic day for our family. Greenville was about 20,000 population and I had never been in any town with more than 3,000 unless it was Tuscaloosa, Alabama, and since I was there at the age of three, I couldn't really remember it. We saw our first steamboat, with its huge paddle wheel at the rear and two huge smokestacks belching out black smoke. The steamboat was tied up to one of the big metal rings anchored in the wharf.

But the river was our main interest. It was said to be ninety-five feet deep at Greenville and if one wanted to cross over into Arkansas, a steamboat in the form of a ferry was used. It would hold about five cars and a hundred or more people, but it took an hour to make the trip across and back. There was no bridge on the Mississippi south of Memphis in 1925, the year of our trip.

I asked Uncle Earl how wide the river really was at that point.

He said, "About a mile."

I said, "It doesn't look that wide to me. How can you tell how wide it is?"

He said he had found that the best way to judge the width of the river was to turn one's back to the river, bend down and look between one's legs. That offered no problem to us boys, but my mother and sisters all had on long dresses, so they had a hard time holding up their skirts and looking between their legs, but they did it. Sure enough, the river looked much wider, but I have often thought how silly we must have looked all lined up with our backs to the river and looking between our legs. When we straightened up Uncle Earl was bent over from laughing at the sight of us. We then found he meant his suggestion as just a big joke.

The trip to the river was a big day in our lives, because it was our first look at the mighty Mississippi, but it wasn't to be our last. Only two years later it came lapping up to our door although we lived 35 miles away.

Mr. Starke, our grade-school principal, was a tall, very slender man of about forty-five. No doubt he was a good principal or he wouldn't have held his job so long. He was a disciplinarian of the old school and every student knew it. To be sent to his office was a humiliating and frightening event. He used to paddle liberally, and for all I know, justly. Mr. Starke was a very solemn man and I don't think he ever smiled. He might compliment a student in a very matter of fact way, but wouldn't smile when doing it. He never raised his voice. It was his usual practice to walk around inspecting the classrooms and what was going on in them while swinging an old fashioned watch fob around his finger. He swung that fob so much that I often wondered if he ever wore out the chain to which it was attached. He kept his pocket watch in a vest pocket and that watch dictated the time he rang all bells.

I didn't really dislike Mr. Starke but he wasn't the kind of principal one could feel close to. Maybe that was just as well. Keeping his distance both from kids and teachers alike may have been best if he were to have a good, disciplined school such as he always had.

Every morning we met in the auditorium for a short devotional service (this was the normal practice for southern schools in what was known as the Bible Belt) and for all announcements of the day. There were no loudspeaker systems over which announcements might be made. This Monday morning in early May was no exception; we met in the auditorium. It was the year 1927.

After the devotional service and some usual announcements regarding school for the day, Mr. Starke said he had a very important announcement but that we must not be upset by it.

He said, "I had a telephone call a few minutes ago from the United States Engineers saying the levee on the Mississippi River had broken near Shaw and the river was rapidly washing out the levee and nearby countryside."

For a few seconds one could have heard a pin drop. Those school kids had never been as quiet in their lives. But after a moment, bedlam broke loose. Everyone present had a question to ask and everyone tried to get Mr. Starke's attention. He banged a gavel on the lectern from which he was speaking and finally got order.

He proceeded in a very normal voice, "We will continue school throughout the week and when we see signs of the flood arriving there will be plenty of time to dismiss school and everyone can go home."

This certainly didn't answer our questions. We were just kids and didn't really know anything about floods. It was forty-five miles to the point where the levee had broken but we could imagine a wall of water coming our way just any day. All sorts of questions began to pound in our heads. How high will the water get? Will it get in our houses? Will we have time to escape to the hill country thirty miles to the east? What becomes of our pets and livestock? We didn't get any satisfactory answers from anything Mr. Starke said. In fact, we didn't get any dependable answers from anyone. Even the Corps of Engineers couldn't predict the exact area where the flood would cover the land. After all, there had been no general flood from the Mississippi River in more than thirty years on the Mississippi side of the river where we lived.

About 200 of us had arrived at school on school buses the morning of the levee break. All of us knew there was a danger of a flood and newspaper reports were scary. The Mississippi River had been rising for weeks. First, it filled its own channel, which was about one mile wide. Then the water began to rise up the sides of the levees, which were as much as forty feet high in places. The levee in Greenville was higher than most of the houses in town. Greenville had an extra levee around the town to protect it from the land side of the river. National Guardsmen were called out to guard the levees. There were attempts by people in Arkansas and Louisiana to dynamite and blow out the levees on the Mississippi side to take the water pressure off their own levees. I suspect some Mississippians probably did the same. In any case, no levees were blown up. "Old Man River" took care of destroying the levees without any help by dynamite.

From Monday through Thursday of that week we continued to ride the bus to school, but I doubt that we learned much because our thoughts were always on the coming flood. Lots of kids and their parents had already boarded trains or cars and headed for the hills to the east. Most families had relatives in east Mississippi or Alabama, as most came from there when they moved to the Delta, just like the Ferguson family.

On Tuesday of that exciting week, the Corps of Engineers put a bulletin in the Memphis newspaper, the *Commercial Appeal*, saying the flood would cover all the land in the area where we lived except for railroad or public road embankments. They thought the water would average being only about two feet deep in the country for miles around. My dad had faith that the Corps of Engineers knew best. After all, they were engineers and had control over all the navigable rivers in the United States.

Since he believed they knew what they were talking about, we set about plans for not evacuating to the hill country. We would just ride out the flood at home and take our chances.

Our barn had a large hay loft. We moved the bales of hay to one corner and swept the loft floors. A hole was cut in the wall near the top of the roof and a stove pipe inserted so that we could move our cookstove up there. If the water rose steadily and we could tell that it would get over the floors of our house, all our furniture could be carried to the barn within hours. But what about the mules, our two cows, the chickens, and pigs?

We built a platform about three feet high and put a fence around it for the pigs. The barn had a large lean-to on the west side. My father put a floor in it about four feet high and built a ramp up to the floor. This was planned for the cows and the mules. We struggled for hours training them to go up and down the ramps in case the water were to cover the barnyard. We were to turn the chickens loose to get to the railroad embankment about 150 feet in front of our house. By feeding them on the railroad they would not stray far away. We knew no trains would be running if the flood covered the land, as some bridges would either be washed out or weakened by the high water.

In addition to preparation for the animals on our farm and the possibility of our having to move to the loft of the barn, we had to have some method of moving around. Papa solved that in about two days. We already had one row boat and he built another and had it finished with time to spare. He worked night and day as did all of us except those in school. There was plenty of work for all and through it all there was worry about how high the water would really get.

All houses in the Delta were built on foundations from one and one half to two feet high and ours was no exception. This was because of moisture. We could not have basements in our area for the same reason. A basement could only add to our problem if the flood came. But when was it coming, if ever?

During the night on Thursday things began to happen, but we didn't know about it at our home. There was no radio and the newspaper information was always about one day behind the times. On Friday, we boarded the school bus as usual, but on the way to school we had to cross two small bayous which led into small rivers. As we crossed them we noted the water in them was higher than usual and running backward from its normal direction. This was scary because we didn't know how fast the water might be rising.

By the time we got to school things were a little bit panicky. The bell rang and we were quickly assembled in the auditorium. There was no devotional or prayer period that morning. Mr. Starke had no trouble getting our attention.

He said "Most of you know the water is coming at last. Moorhead Bayou is almost bank-full and running backward. Go to your desks and remove everything you own. The buses will be ready to board within thirty minutes and a count will be taken to be sure everyone is accounted for."

Actually, more than half the kids and their families had already headed for the hills and the bus was only about half full. As we started home none of us knew how high the water might get or how long we would be out of school. Everything was at the mercy of the flooding Mississippi.

The next two weeks were an exciting time for me. The water rose higher and higher. We had a beautiful potato crop for our own use but the water soon covered the plants and killed them. We had tried to build a small levee around the potatoes by using plows and tamping the loose dirt down, but wave action washed out the low levee and the potatoes suffered a watery death.

After about four days all our land was covered and the water was within about one inch of our floors when it ceased rising. Everybody was happy about that. It meant we would not have to move to the barn loft. We tied our boats up to the front porch, but Hubert and I used them for good purposes elsewhere.

In the woods, the birds weren't bothered, and neither were the squirrels, which ate bugs and leaves on the trees. Anyway, they could go from tree to tree without getting wet. But the poor rabbits had a tough time. As Hubert and I paddled through the woods we noted lots of rabbits were marooned on floating logs with nothing to eat. So we started catching them and placing them in a cage we carried in the boat. They would try to escape us in fear, but we could catch them when they were swimming. In this manner we caught dozens of them and put them on the railroad embankment where they had lots of grass and weeds for cover and food.

One day some boys from town came down the railroad and were throwing rocks at the rabbits. Of course, the rabbits had no way to escape without swimming away and if they did that they would surely drown. My dad got out his old ten-gauge shotgun and fired two shots into the air. He yelled a warning for the boys to go back to town and leave the rabbits alone. We never saw them again. No doubt they had a little fear of what my dad might have done with the shotgun if they hadn't abided by his warning.

One night when the flood was at its highest point a severe lightning and wind storm came up. The waves got pretty high and beat against the walls of the house. This didn't do any harm, but the water did start coming through the cracks around the doorways. We all got brooms and mops and kept it out the best we could, but at one time the water was about two inches deep in the house. Then the storm abated as suddenly as it arrived and the water calmed down. Finally, when we saw there was no danger from the water we all went to bed and slept like logs from exhaustion.

The next morning I awoke with the sun shining brightly. I went to the front screen door and looked out across the porch. Lying on the edge of the porch, level with my feet, was a huge water moccasin, a dreaded cottonmouth. He seemed sound asleep, enjoying the sunshine. I eased over to the closet where a .22 rifle was leaning against the wall, pumped a shell into the firing chamber and then tip-toed back to the front door. My plan was to open the door just an inch or two and then shoot the snake's head. With the gun cocked I gently opened the door, but the darn thing squeaked. The snake must have been sleeping very lightly because he sensed the squeak, opened his eyes in alarm, and rolled off into the water without my being able to get a shot at him.

We kept asking ourselves where all the snakes were coming from. Floods don't produce snakes, but we found that floods flush them out of holes in the ground, hollow logs, or any other place they usually hide or live. They must have been all around us in the woods and weeds without our knowing so many were present. As Hubert and I paddled our boat through the woods looking for rabbits to rescue, we could always see a snake swimming somewhere, so we set about snake hunting.

We had a wooden handled implement with a curved blade on its end. It was known as a Kaiser Blade and was used in cutting small bushes, vines, and saplings. We armed ourselves with Kaiser Blades and then paddled through the woods. We would paddle quickly up to a swimming snake and with a mighty swing of the Kaiser Blade separate him into two parts. No doubt about it: we lowered the snake population quite a lot in that manner. Of course, it was only the moccasins we were after as the other snakes, except rattlers, were not harmful, and we saw no rattlers. They must have been on or in floating logs, as they swim only when forced to do so.

All victims of the flood didn't get off as easily as we did. Of course, it ruined the crops already planted, but at least it didn't harm our house or any of the tenant houses on our farm. Nobody on our farm had a real shortage of food. The government sent loads of food out along the railroads by small gasoline-propelled cars that pulled other very small carts behind them. We bought the things we had to have, but this could not have gone on very long as no one's diet was really a balanced one. There were almost no vegetables. People who lived near the river had a really tough time of it. Of course, most of them evacuated their homes as water was quite often up to the eaves. In Greenville, the water was fifteen to twenty feet deep and lots of houses floated off their foundations and ended up in clusters of eight or ten homes jammed together. After the flood some were moved back to their foundations.

All things were not drudgery or dull during the flood. Hubert and I paddled our boat miles and miles going to other houses to be sure people had enough to eat and were not sick. But one little adventure almost put an end to us when we least expected it.

The flood water was always trying to make its way to lower ground at the south end of the Delta ninety miles away at Vicksburg. There it would go back into the Mississippi River as its crest receded. This meant that all east and west railroad embankments held up the progress of the flood. The water on the north side of the railroad was about a foot higher than on the south side where our house was located. There was a concrete culvert four feet in diameter under the railroad about one quarter of a mile from our house. Water gushed through this huge culvert at tremendous speed under high pressure. This water had a strong current for about 100 to where there was a barbed-wire fence along the roadway. Hubert and I decided we would paddle just as fast as we could along the railroad embankment at the mouth of the gushing culvert and try to get across the speeding current before it could sweep us away to the south and into the barbed-wire fence.

We gave ourselves about a hundred feet to gain our fastest speed. We paddled furiously, but it was to no avail. Instead of crossing the gushing current, no sooner than our boat hit it, we lost control and were propelled sideways. Although we paddled as hard as we could there was no way to get out of the rushing current. There was nothing to do except let the current take over. It did for certain, and within a few seconds we were lodged helplessly against the barb wire fence. As soon as we hit the fence sideways the boat began to fill with water. Down we went with the boat, but of course it didn't really sink to the ground underneath as the boat was made of light pine wood. Also the water was only about four feet deep.

The only escape was for us to jump into the raging current, and while holding to the wire try to work the boat alongside the fence. It was slow work and we tore our clothes on the barbs and got a few skin punctures also. Even when we got free, we had a boat full of water and no way to empty it. At a very slow pace we made our way along the fence, pulling the water-logged boat along.

When we finally got the boat home Papa was waiting for us. I doubt that he needed to tell us never to try that trick again but he told us anyway. The truth is we had learned our lesson at small cost: a few scratches and some torn clothes.

On the thirteenth day the water began to recede rapidly. When it was gone from our area all the land was covered with about a half an inch of silt that made our land still more fertile than it was before. It made us keenly aware that it was by flooding periodically over many thousands of years that the Delta soil had been formed in the first place. It was this silt that made it some of the most fertile soil in the world, rich in nitrogen and free of rocks. And, although late starting, our crops were highly productive the year of the great flood. We had seen a world of water although 35 miles away from its source, the mighty Mississippi.

Thankfully, the Mississippi River has never flooded as extensively since 1927 and the levees have always been equal to their task.

Chapter 11

DELTA WATERS

"Wilson, you have to be the first to dive in, it's your turn to be first," was my older brother Hubert's orders.

In ordinary swimming pools that might be a privilege, but not when one was diving into a stagnant pool of water in a drainage ditch, where snakes, frogs, tadpoles, and fish were found in large numbers.

Drainage ditches, known to us as dredge ditches, were necessary in the Mississippi Delta country, where the land was flat for miles and rainfall was very plentiful. In winter the ditches ran full, draining excess water off the crop land, but in the long, hot, dry summers, the water dried up except for deep holes of water usually found where the ditches ran through woods or swamps. The hole we planned to swim in was one of those holes.

Our town didn't have a public swimming pool in that year, 1928, so we swam in these dredge ditch holes. This particular one was about twenty-five feet across and fifty yards long. Thorny blackberry vines and small willows grew down to the water's edge. A large sycamore tree had fallen across this pool of water years before. Now the bark was off it and it was slick and difficult for one to stand on and keep his balance. Sitting on it and dangling one's feet in the muddy water was no problem. With those thorny vines along the bank we always took off our clothes, piled them at the base of the log and walked gingerly out on the log. Modesty didn't require any swimming suits there as it was about half a mile to the nearest cotton field and a mile to the nearest home.

Of course, the first diver made as big a splash as he could so as to scare the snakes and frogs out. Snakes and frogs don't like to share a swimming hole with a bunch of noisy, splashing boys, and boys have the same feeling about snakes. The only water snakes in that area of the Delta were brown water snakes and cotton-mouth moccasins. Those brown water snakes were not supposed to have poison in their fangs, but their fangs were always so dirty and germ-ridden that when bitten by one, a few days in the hospital could be expected as a result. Cottonmouth moccasins were an entirely different story. They had triangular heads, the inside of their mouths were white (that's why the cottonmouth name), and they were longer and not as big around the middle as the brown water snakes. They had deadly poison in their fangs and they resented being disturbed by anything. A bite from one of them put Freddie Tyler, a friend, in the hospital for weeks. At one time, his hand, upon which he was bitten, was almost amputated as a result. Freddie had been bitten while hand fishing.

So it was with some fear and misgivings that I dived in with a big splash and swam the length of the pool and back, making all the noise I could and dog paddling as fast as I could. Returning to the log, I climbed up and sat on it.

Sure enough, we began seeing crawling snakes and jumping frogs getting out of the pool and leaving it to us. The snakes, in my imagination, looked angry about having to leave their watery haven, but the frogs hopped along and up into the bushes as if it was no bother. No doubt they got just far enough into the bushes and briars to be hidden from our view, but close enough to know when we left.

Once we felt we had the pool to ourselves we began diving, swimming and returning to the log for a rest. All of us could dog paddle and kick like frogs, but only one could do the Australian Crawl, a new swimming stroke that had just been invented and was used by some Olympic swimmers of that day. This particular crawl and flutter-kick was a new thing and we watched Genie Jones do it. He had been away at Scout Camp and the swimming instructor had taught it to him. On this day it was to come in handy as he could swim much faster than those of us who could only dog paddle, or crawl with the froglike kick.

After swimming awhile and then resting on the log, Hubert told us he thought he had seen a cottonmouth moccasin poke his head above the water near a small bush at the far end of the pond.

"Aw, you're just seeing things," Genie told him. "It was probably only a floating chip of wood. I'll just swim down there and scare him away, but all the snakes are up there in the bushes looking at us, hoping we'll soon leave so they can come back into the water. There's no snake up there."

Genie swam so gracefully down to the end of the pool that all of us were envious. He turned near the end, and with a big flutter-kick started back.

As he made his first kick to turn, his foot hit something in the water and he yelled, "Snake! I kicked a snake and he almost wrapped his body around my leg. It must be that cottonmouth."

It's too bad we didn't have some way to time Genie's return to the safety of the log because we thought for years afterward that he had set a new record for fifty yards. That mad cottonmouth followed Genie about half way to the log and then stopped on top of the water almost in a coil. His long tongue flicked out in anger and he remained there. We had nothing to throw at him and all decided it was time to give the pond back to the "king" of the pool.

The events of this Sunday were not over by any means. Just as we were dressing, we heard a train whistle and knew instantly that it was the two p.m. passenger train on the C. & G. Railroad about two miles north of us. It told us we were much, much too late in getting home from Sunday School and church where we were supposed to be.

On that Sunday morning, Hubert and I had started walking to town about three miles away by railroad track, a track we walked many times. Mother and Papa did not go that day. We had no car at the time and it was too much to expect Mother to walk six miles just to get to church and back.

When about half-way to town we met Bill Thomas, Maxwell Tolar, and Genie Jones coming out of town and also walking the track.

"Where are you guys going?" Hubert asked.

"To the swimming hole in the woods about a mile north of your house," Bill said. He also asked us why we didn't skip church and go with them.

"Genie has a new swimming stroke he wants to show us," he said.

I could almost see the wheels turning in Hubert's head. He knew he should go to church, but he wanted to go swimming much more than he wanted to go and sit in that hot church. I didn't say a word, but secretly I wanted to go swimming and waited anxiously for his answer.

"We sure could get in big trouble if the folks found out, you know," Hubert said in a weakening kind of way.

"Aw, nobody has to know, we will get out of the swimming hole in plenty of time. You can then get back on the railroad and walk home as if nothing had happened," Bill argued.

I guess this logic won Hubert over, and you can be sure I wasn't going to church by myself. What we were doing was almost unthinkable because we never violated our parents' trust that I can remember, except that one time. Perhaps we did one other time when we climbed the hawk-nest tree. So that is how we got to the swimming hole and became interested in our fun that we didn't have any thought of time passing until too late.

When the whistle blew we knew almost for certain that we would be found out. It was at least an hour after we were due home and it would require at least a half an hour to get home after dressing.

After dressing as hurriedly as possible, we started through the woods. As we entered the open cotton field between the woods and our house, there stood Papa waiting for us. On the way he had cut a bundle of willow limbs and stripped them off for switches.

For what seemed like forever, he just stood there looking at us. He didn't ask for any excuses and we didn't give any. Why? Because we didn't have any to give. To play hooky from church was worse to some than playing hooky from school, but never, never, had we played hooky from school.

" Which one of you wants it first?" my father asked.

"I do," I said.

It was no use in delaying and I just thought it best to get it over with. He bent me over and really applied those willow limbs with force. They stung my backside something awful and made my skin rise in welts but I didn't cry. What was the use in crying? I just stood the pain and knew it would be over soon. Then he whipped Hubert next and I'm sorry to say, I think he whipped him harder and longer than he did me. Maybe it was because he thought I would never have skipped church except to follow Hubert. Anyway, that is the way I thought of it at the time. Later, Hubert and I recounted what had happened and knew that was the last time he ever whipped us. Maybe it was a good lesson.

On the way home nothing was said. Nothing needed to be said. The story was already over for that Sunday and you can bet we never played hooky from church again. I'm sure Papa told Mother about what happened but the event was never mentioned, not even in front of my smaller brothers, Louis or Paul.

Anyone who has been around the numerous lakes and bayous of the Mississippi Delta knows they are inhabited by snakes, turtles, frogs and fish. Some of those fish are gars, of which there are two kinds. One is known as a pike gar. It is very long, almost like a pencil, and isn't considered edible. The other is known as an alligator gar, thick in body and usually much shorter than the pike gar. We saw very few alligator gars but there were many, many pike gars. In the very south end of the Delta near Vicksburg there were some real alligators, but they did not invade our lakes and chose to stay in the warmer water of the lakes farther south.

The alligator gar had eyes located in knots on the top of his head and broad jaws with flaring teeth on each side, somewhat like an alligator. It was because of the looks of his head and the very heavy scales on his body that this fish became known as an alligator gar.

My dad always said that alligator gar meat would be good enough to eat in view of the fact that we were in need of meat more often than we could get it. One of these alligator gars played a large part, almost a tragic part, in one of our outings for meat.

It happened during the great depression which one reads about in history books now-a-days and which grandparents talk about in telling stories of the 1930s. Food was scarce, especially meat, but even if there had been plenty of meat there was almost no money with which to buy it. People supplemented their meager supplies with fish when it could be had. Seining for fish was one way to do this.

About two miles east of our home was a small lake known as Long Lake although it was only about half a mile long and 150 yards wide. It held lots of fish such as buffalo and catfish, along with some speckled perch and bream. In summer, the lake was never more than five feet deep and therefore easy to seine as one could wade everywhere and still keep his head above water.

We bought a seine from the Sears Roebuck catalogue and it was sent out from the big Sears store in Memphis. Our plan was to catch all the fish we could and distribute them to people living all around, but mostly to the Negro tenant farmers who lived on our farm. But you can be sure we wanted some of them for ourselves because we were short on meat just as everyone else was.

Seining Long Lake would not have been all that exciting except for an unfounded rumor that was making the rounds with the Negro tenant farmers. Someone who had gone swimming in Long Lake had said they saw a huge gar sunning himself on top of the water. They said his eyes bulged on the top of his head like those of an alligator and that the gar was as long as a man. By the time the story had made its rounds and reached us, one might have thought the gar was ten feet long and would weigh 200 pounds or more. The story, true or not, made this particular seining trip more exciting. We didn't really believe the story, but we couldn't completely dismiss it from our minds.

So, on the appointed day, we loaded up two wagons with about twelve of us, along with the seine. At least five of the twelve were blacks, who worked and lived on our farm as sharecroppers. One of the blacks was named Joe McMillan. He didn't work as a sharecropper; he worked as a day laborer for my father. To tell the truth, he was more of a right hand man for my father than any of us boys. Being young and just married with no children, he was a sort of carefree spirit. Riding innocently along in the wagon, Joe had no idea of the terrifying experience he was to have that day.

While on the way to the lake I noticed that my father had put a sledgehammer and his .38 caliber Smith and Wesson pistol near the seine.

I asked him, "Papa, why are you taking your pistol and ax and sledgehammer along? We're not going to build any fences or shoot any wild game."

He replied, "You never can tell when they might come in handy."

Then the thought hit me that it might be he believed the gar stories going around.

We arrived at the lake, unloaded and straightened the seine and prepared for seining for fish. The plan was to tie one end of the seine to the bank and then string out the rest of the seine across the lake as far as it might reach. The end of the seine in the lake was pulled into a semi-circle and was weighted by lead sinkers and the top was held up by wood floats. We thought no fish could escape.

Although no one said anything about it, we were all keeping wary eyes out for a huge gar that might become encircled by the seine.

When everything was set, with the two strong men holding the end of the seine out in the lake, all the remaining people, blacks and whites, kids and adults, went about 150 yards above the seine and waded out into the lake very quietly. Each had a board or stick in his hand. At a given signal from my father, we all shouted and slapped the water with the sticks and waded or swam as fast as possible toward the seine. All this commotion was supposed to scare the fish toward the net and, as quickly as possible, the end of the seine out in the lake was pulled to the shore. Inside this circle, after both ends were pulled to the shore, was, we hoped, a large number of fish.

The fish were there, because we could see them making the water boil, but then we were startled by a huge wave made by something as it swam along the inside of the seine. No doubt it was looking for a hole or a place to escape its encirclement.

My dad yelled, "Boys, it must be the alligator gar. It will tear a hole in our seine just as soon as it wants to!"

His prediction came true.

This fish, which we had not yet seen, swam hurriedly over to the seine near the shore as if to beach himself, and then reversed course and headed for deeper water. The water boiled almost like a miniature submarine taking off at full speed toward the surrounding seine. It seemed the wave was heading straight toward my father, who was against the outside of the seine in about five feet of water.

I yelled, "Look out, Papa, he's heading straight for you!"

But it was too late. The unseen fish hit the net and tore it to shreds and then glanced off my father's leg as he headed for freedom. That's when we knew it was an alligator gar. How did we know? Well, those curling teeth had torn my father's overalls and had cut the skin of his leg as if you had pulled a saw across it. It wasn't a serious wound. We poured some iodine on it, tied a rag around it, and he went on about seining.

As we pulled the seine into a tight circle on the bank, it soon became evident that all of the good fish we had circled, such as buffalo and catfish, were escaping through the giant hole the gar had made in the net. All hands were more excited about the size of the giant gar than about losing the fish which were so important as food.

What to do about it was the question. My father soon put an end to our speculation. He said, "We will repair the net and try to encircle him again. But this time, we will always have the net loose, so that when he hits it with his snout, it will not be taut and easily broken. If we have it loose, he will get himself wrapped up in it and then, maybe, we can subdue him with my pistol or that sledgehammer."

So we cut the seine into two pieces and tied the ends together with some of the shredded cords the gar had broken. Also, we borrowed a boat from the owner of the lake and had the pistol and sledgehammer in it.

Once again, we put the seine out in its semi-circle fashion with one end tied to the bank and, once again, we went into the lake to scare the fish into the net. Only this time we went down the lake where the gar had gone with the water cascading over his back and his tail fin slashing the water like the propeller of a boat.

All the while we were asking each other, "How big do you think he is? What happens to me if he heads in my direction?" Now we were all scared of him. What took place in the next fifteen minutes justified our fright.

We kept the net slack, as we had planned, but this time, there were four of the black men behind the net; that is, outside of the circle of the net. My father remained in the boat inside the circle, armed with the pistol and sledgehammer. Of course, at first we didn't know if the gar had gone into the net, but our suspense was ended in about a minute after the outer end of the seine was pulled to shore.

Suddenly, there was a swirl of water in the middle of the circle and a big wave, as the gar made a tight turn and headed for the net. He had gotten out once and it may be he thought a hard charge of the net would allow him to escape again.

He headed for the net at full speed, causing the water to rise over his back. This time he hit the net at a slack place, but on the opposite side of the net was Joe McMillan up to his neck in the five foot deep water. The gar, with the net around his snout, hit Joe in the middle of the stomach and he went under, leaving his hat floating on the surface where he had been seconds before. Almost in an instant, Joe came to the top for air, but he, the gar and the net became a boiling mass, as the huge gar fought Joe and the net to escape.

My father, seeing what was happening, began paddling the boat to the spot as fast as possible. In the meantime, Joe was trying to hold onto the gar, yet escape drowning. He would go under then force himself up to the surface for air; the gar with the net wrapped around him all the while.

"Hurry up, Mr. Ferguson, he's drowning me!" he yelled.

"Hold on, Joe! I'll be there in a minute!" my father yelled back at Joe.

We couldn't believe what we were seeing. The gar was bigger and longer than Joe McMillan and he was thrashing around something awful. Finally, my father arrived at the struggle. He raised his sledgehammer and slugged the gar on the head as Joe came up for air with him. But this blow seemed to only anger him. He thrashed harder and harder and we began to worry about Joe drowning, so we yelled for him to turn loose and save himself. To this day, I can't understand why that small black man continued to hold the struggling gar.

Then the fireworks began. My dad pulled his pistol out of the holster and each time Joe pulled the gar to the surface, my father fired into the gar's head, being careful to avoid hitting Joe. He fired time after time, not always hitting his target. But after about five shots, the gar began to weaken and soon he ceased to struggle. Then, for the first time, we knew we had him for good. A half-drowned Joe McMillan was still holding the tremendous gar in his arms with the net of the seine still around the gar. We pulled Joe into the boat because he was too weak to wade to shore. Joe collapsed in the bottom of the boat in his near-drowned state and the first thing he wanted was his straw hat which was still floating on the water about twenty-five yards away.

By this time the sound of the pistol shots and news of the struggle had spread to the houses around the edge of the lake and a small crowd had gathered to see what was going on. They saw the largest gar any of them had seen in their lives. Scales, normally used in weighing sacks of cotton, were hung from a nearby tree limb and the gar weighed and measured. We couldn't believe it at first, but this mammoth alligator gar weighed 117 pounds and was four-feet, eleven inches long. Of course, fish much larger grow in the ocean but who could have believed a fish so large could grow in a small lake only about half a mile long and 200 wide?

Gar meat certainly wasn't the tastiest fish one finds in lakes such as Long Lake, but it was very edible in those days when meat of any sort was so difficult to buy, and so we set about dressing him. We sliced the hull down the bottom side from head to tail by using an ax and then peeled the hull back, uncovering the huge body of the gar. When his entrails were removed, we then cut his large body into chunks about four inches long. We handed them out to all the helpers and they cut those chunks into gar steaks. Mother cut our steaks into small pieces, dipped them in corn meal and fried them to a crisp brown. That time, gar meat tasted almost as good as fresh perch.

After the struggle with the gar and the work in dressing him, the entire crew was so tired that we decided to do no more seining that day. We headed the wagons toward home without the buffalo and catfish we had come for, but with some pretty good meat from the largest fish any of us had ever seen.

What could farm families do for excitement after the crops were "laid by" in the summer? "Laid by" meant that all row crops had been cultivated the last time and that there was a three or four week interval before they were ready to harvest. We spent some of that time cutting wood for winter. This meant we still had one or two weeks to take things easy. Of course, Papa could always have us shucking corn in the corn crib if he could find nothing else for us to do.

There was no way we could go to the Gulf Coast or to Colorado, or to any other place very far away, because of the lack of money and because we were a large family. And, too, most of the time we had no car. But we still had a good time by taking a camping-out trip that is hard to believe in these days of campers, sleeping bags, portable stoves, etc. Our trip took lots of planning and a willingness, on our part, to be somewhat uncomfortable.

We wanted to go to One Mile Lake, which was about five miles away. Part of the way was by road, either dirt or gravel, and the remainder, only a trail in the woods for about a mile to the bank of the lake. Our spot was to be under a huge oak tree, which played an important part in one of the exciting events that happened to us.

We had a tent, which we ordered from Sears Roebuck catalogue. It lasted for several years and was quite big, let's say about twelve by twenty feet. There were two tent poles and numerous pegs, which we used to fasten down the sides. Our transportation was by wagon and it was pulled by two mules. The side boards were placed on the wagon so the sides would be high enough to hold everything we needed. We took two or three mattresses and two cots for our parents to sleep on. The mattresses were to be laid on the ground for us kids. We also took two kerosene lanterns and food which could be cooked over a campfire. Poor Mother, she had to stoop over that hot fire for two days. Feed for the mules, a keg of water, and a 100 pound block of ice wrapped in quilts were also taken along. We got the ice from the ice truck, which came by our farm two days a week. Of course, we took all the milk we could and kept it from curdling for about two days by storing it next to the huge block of ice.

When loaded with all of our supplies, five kids and our parents, the wagon was full to the top and almost overflowing. Off we went, and it was difficult to be patient and wait for the three-hour wagon trip to pass. The road through the woods was rough, but the spot beside the lake was so pretty that the discomfort of riding in a rough wagon was quickly forgotten after we arrived. Everyone had something to do to put up the tent and get supplies in order. We took a quick look at the lake, after running about sixty yards to its edge. Woods surrounded the lake on both sides and no one lived closer than about a mile away. I guess that is why the poachers had nerve enough to do what they had done to the lake.

We yelled for our father to come quickly and take a look. Large fish, both gar and buffalo, were at the top, swimming feebly with their noses out of the water in an attempt to get air. My father recognized what had happened immediately. He said someone had limed the lake just before our arrival. I have never seen such a thing, except that day on the shore of One Mile Lake. Fish were swimming all over. There is a kind of lime to which water must be added in order for it to harden into cement. In the process of mixing with water, a large amount of the oxygen in the lake water is absorbed, leaving too little for the fish to breath. As a result, they come to the top seeking oxygen. The poachers did this dirty trick by paddling a boat from one end of the lake to the other and sloshing a gunny sack containing unslacked lime up and down as they paddled. My father said this doesn't usually kill the fish, but they are forced to come to the surface, where they are easily caught in a dipnet. Our arrival scared the poachers off. No doubt, they had expected to catch hundreds of pounds of fish and sell them at the fish market in Moorhead.

The fish continued their desperate search for air for quite a while, until a strong breeze came up, causing waves about three or four inches high. This wave action caused the water to absorb more oxygen and the fish could then breath more naturally. After an hour or two , they disappeared from the surface and we found none of them dead. I wanted to catch a couple of the large buffalo for us to have a fish fry, but my dad said "nothing doing" to that suggestion. He said it was just too unsportsmanlike and we would have no part of it. I guess he was right, but I sure did like buffalo dipped in corn meal and fried. I think my dad was pretty sure we could get some fresh fish the legal way.

Soon after our arrival, some of us took a short ride in a boat we had arranged to use. It was already tied to a sapling at the bank. We paddled for a while looking the lake over, and then tied it up again, but not very well, as we were to find out later.

I don't think we kids slept well that night because a younger brother had just read a magazine article on snakes. He said rattlesnakes like to crawl into bed with someone sleeping on the ground, in order to share some of the person's body heat. You can imagine what that did to us on our first night in camp. We finally went to sleep with the distant sound of owls hooting back and forth, giving each other some message which we couldn't understand.

The next morning dawned bright and sunny, and we expected to go swimming in the lake that day. I decided to take a stroll down to the boat as Mother was cooking oatmeal and scrambling eggs on the campfire. What did I see? The boat had slipped its moorings during the night and it was now lodged against a submerged log about forty yards out from shore. I yelled for help and my father and brothers came running to see what had happened.

What could we do? I was the oldest boy on the trip and the only one who could swim at all—I had learned to swim the summer before in the great flood. My father never did learn to swim. I always wondered why, when he grew up on a farm in Alabama. Whatever the reason, he couldn't swim a lick and we couldn't think of any way to retrieve the boat, except for me to swim out and paddle it to shore.

At first, my dad just said the boat could stay there, that he wouldn't have me risk my life swimming out to get it when there was no one to help me in case I got cramps or couldn't make it to the boat. Truthfully, I wasn't worried a bit about being able to swim to the boat. I said I would first wade out as far as possible, then push off the bottom and dog paddle until I got there. There was quite a family conference about this. Mother came down to the lake and she had her say along with everyone else. Finally, I convinced them it was safe, but only after my father had found a very dry piece of a large log. He knew it would float very high in the water and would support me if I needed to hang on to it. He said it was so dry and light, that he would wade out as far as he could with the floating chunk of log beside him. Then, I was to push off the bottom and go as fast as I could, but if I should have trouble, or get too tired, he would try to throw the floating chunk near me, so I might use it as a float.

Finally, the moment to try came and I pushed off. Really, it was a simple thing to do. I swam as hard as I could, but wasn't tired at all when I reached the boat, pulled myself over the side, and paddled it back to shore. After that all of us were careful to tie the boat securely at the shore. We had learned our lesson.

The next night in camp, all of us had a new experience. That is, all except my father. He said that when it became dark, he would call up the owls in the surrounding woods and get them to gather in the huge oak tree over our campsite. We boys looked at each other in disbelief. Could he really do it? For most of the late afternoon, that was the big subject for conversation and we waited anxiously for nightfall. After a seemingly interminable time of waiting, the sun finally set and darkness crept up to our campsite.

Certain things had to be done first. The campfire had to be out, so that no coals or flames could be seen. The lanterns hanging on the tent poles for light had to be snuffed out and everybody had to get still and quiet. But what could we do about the mules? They snort and nicker just like horses and there is no way to know when they will do this. So my father took them to a tree about 200 yards away on the side of the lake and tied them to it. Now they were so far away that their nickering wouldn't affect what my father was to try to do.

After a few minutes of waiting, an owl in a tree perhaps a quarter-mile away, deep in the woods, hooted. My father went to the base of a tree and hooted back. He did this by cupping his hands on either side of his mouth. The sound, when put in print, was about like, "Whooo-Whooo-Whooo-Whooo-Whooo-Whooo-Whooo-Whooah." Another owl nearby answered with his hoot. And then still another owl hooted. Between hoots, there would be perhaps two minutes of silence. My father also waited and hooted again. This went on for quite a while with him hooting and the owls replying. I suppose he didn't sound exactly like an owl to the owls, and they got curious about what kind of owl would make a strange hooting sound. Their curiosity got the better of them and they began flying from one tree top to another, always getting closer to the strange "owl" they had never heard before. As for us, we sat as quietly as mice in the pitch darkness.

The owls came closer and closer, hooting each time they landed in a tree top. Then there was quietness and we wondered if they had finally decided the sound they heard was not coming from an owl. Then suddenly we heard the sound of large wings beating the air, after which quiet followed. The next hoot was in the tree directly over my father. Other owls followed and they began hooting back and forth, having a genuine pow-wow over a strange owl being in the forest. Owls can see at night and my father, knowing this, had covered himself with a small tarpaulin. He kept hooting at intervals, until there were about five or six owls in the tree over our campsite.

Having accomplished his purpose, he threw the cover off and we heard owls leaving the tree in a hurry. He had really fooled them. That is the only time I have ever known owls to be called to a certain tree.

Although we didn't get to eat any of the buffalo fish which were on the top of the water when we arrived at the lake, that didn't mean we didn't have fresh fish to eat.

My father knew how to catch bass without a rod and reel, such as everyone fishes with these days and times. We had no rod or reels, but he knew how to catch bass when they were striking surface lures. We had a very long cane pole, to which he tied about twelve feet of cotton line, as monofilament lines had not yet been invented. There were surface lures, which looked almost like the lures now used by all bass fishermen. In summer, the best time to catch bass was just before dark or just before daybreak. At these times, bass would come near the top to strike at and feed on insects that fell into the water from tree limbs or from the air. It was my job to paddle the boat and I had to do this without making a sound, which would spook the fish. I could not allow the paddle to touch or bump the boat. We cruised slowly and soundlessly along near the shore. My father would cast the lure near the bank in the semi-darkness and then pull it with jerks, so that it looked like a bug in distress. A bass hit it with a big splash and hooked himself on the lure's treble hook. Success at last. Then we got the hang of it and before the sun came over the trees on the lake shore, we had pulled in six beautiful bass. Mother dipped them in corn meal and fried them slowly in lard. When they were well done, the bass were delicious. It may be they tasted even better because we had caught them.

Later that day, we made the long trip home and all of us kids were glad to get into our own beds. We had lots to tell our friends about the owls, the boat and the bass in the days to come.

Chapter 12

INNOCENT RACISM

Imagine needing twenty "hands", meaning twenty people old enough and strong enough to do a day's work in the fields, to cultivate 135 acres of cotton, corn, soya beans, and alfalfa. From 1924 until 1940 that is the number we needed to cultivate our farm. At least four of the twenty were always our own family members. The others were blacks from four families. They lived in houses almost like ours, except for being slightly smaller, with none of us having running water, electricity, or any heat other than a cookstove and open fireplace. All, like ours, were built up two feet from ground level on concrete supports so air and chickens could circulate underneath.

Such a large number were needed because everything was done by hand or by mules pulling one-row cultivators or plows. The only chemical used was fertilizer and this was distributed by hand from bags carried on one's shoulders. There were no tractors, no machine cotton pickers, and no airplanes to spread boll weevil poison or other chemicals.

At that time, I never knew a black over twenty-five years of age who had more than four years of grade school work, and the school sessions were only six months long, as any black or white kid over eleven worked in the fields. The younger ones carried water or tools to those working in the fields. Older blacks, almost without exception, could not read or write.

We whites always said the Negroes didn't have any ambition and were satisfied if they had reasonably good health, plenty of food, simple clothes to wear, and a little money to spend on Saturday night when all grown blacks, except the very old, went to town. We could not depend upon them spending their money for the next week's food supply before spending it on themselves or "treating" the ladies and friends. For this reason, my father made up a list of supplies for one week for each family and a wagon pulled by two mules was dispatched to town to haul back the week's "furnish." My father "carried" them on credit all during the growing season and didn't expect repayment until harvest time in the fall. It was the same with my father. He borrowed money from the bank and paid it back in the fall, also. He never charged a Negro family more than six percent interest, no matter what the bank charged him.

My mother had no medical training but she had a medical book somewhat like a Lincoln Library Book in which she read of most diseases common among both blacks and whites of that day. When a black got sick she immediately pulled on her rubber boots, mounted a mule, side-saddle, and went to help. Many times the illness was caused by their not eating correct foods. Pellegra was very common among Negroes and all she had to do was force them to eat turnip greens, which cured it within days. Mother also called on white families too poor to afford a doctor. Most of her calls were in winter when a doctor could not have gotten to the ill due to muddy roads. She also assisted black women in giving birth but no one ever referred to her as a mid-wife. The blacks admired my mother for all she tried to do for them.

There were unwritten social laws governing the relation-ships of whites and Negroes. None of us ever thought of them as laws, or unbreakable customs for that matter. For example: no Negro ever came to our front door. He or she always came to the rear door of our house. If a Negro had important business with my father he entered through the rear door and Papa then invited him into the living room to sit around the fireplace and talk. At the age of eleven, I was addressed as "Mr. Wilson". The same applied to the younger kids. It was always "Miss Clara," "Mr. Lewis," etc. We called them by their first names, such as John, Joe, etc. We knew their last names but they often had four or five names such as George Washington Lincoln Jones. I don't know why but we addressed very old Negroes as "Auntie" or "Uncle." We never shook hands with Negroes and we kids never played ball with them except for "playing catch." We never hunted with them. Mother always thought we would learn to speak their colloquial language and take up too many of their habits and "ways."

I have often tried to explain to my own satisfaction our genuine attitude toward the Negroes who lived on our farm. I'm sure we had a sincere good feeling toward each Negro that worked for us. If one were injured, everyone was truly sorry and wanted to do what could be done to heal the hurt. We could not have stood the idea of any one of them being hungry, and would have given them of our food if they were. Individually, we cared for them deep down inside. We worked alongside them in the fields doing the same work they did. While doing that we enjoyed their singing. It's too bad tape recorders had not yet been invented; if they had been I could have recorded some beautiful harmony. Some of their songs seemed to be chants of some type that were handed down from generation to generation from their days as slaves and even before that when they lived in Africa, and many were religious in nature. I always thought they could sing "Tenting Tonight" better than the writer even thought it could be sung. Of course, that had to do with the Civil War.

Our Negro families were free to move from our farm to some other farm at the end of the crop season, but my father had such a good reputation among Negroes that we almost never had a family wish to move. In fact, many more applied to my father than he could ever have room for. All white farm owners didn't have that reputation and I'm sure that's putting it pretty mildly.

I clearly remember a family living about half a mile up the road toward Moorhead. They were hard workers, but had no money to call a doctor. They became violently ill with an intestinal disorder and very high fever. All members of the family except for the father and one little girl were dreadfuly ill. When Mother heard about them, she got out her medical book and went to see them. I was so proud of her later when the doctor who did finally treat them said that she had correctly diagnosed their illness as typhoid fever. When she felt sure that was the problem she had every dish, drinking cup, and cloth in the house boiled in a metal washpot out in the yard. She had the whole house disinfected with something like Lysol. With the help of the medical doctor they recovered and the father and little girl never became ill.

Were Negroes oppressed in those days? We didn't think so. We thought they were happy and contented. No other thought ever entered our minds. My father was a little ahead of his time in telling others that we should have better schools for the Negroes. He always argued that if all Negroes became literate, they would want to better their standard of living, and as better consumers, everyone would benefit. But his ideas fell on deaf ears. Negro schools improved only very gradually until the U.S. Supreme Court rulings were handed down many years later. Then vast changes came about and with them, severe social upheavals. The beginning of the unbelievable changes all started when one little black lady refused to give up her seat in the bus in Montgomery, Alabama, and move to the "black section."

In the 1920's the make-up of Negro families changed often. Lots of men and women married often, but almost never bothered with divorce as divorces were expensive, requiring lawyers and court costs. An example is that of Joe McMillan, the black man who almost drowned while helping us capture an alligator gar.   One day I noted that Joe was listless and despondent.   His wife, Mary, had left him, taking all her belongings. She didn't even say goodbye. They had no children. After a few days, I decided to talk to Joe about his problem.

When I asked him how he felt he said, "Mr. Wilson, I feel just like a wagon wheel with about half its spokes broken out."

Later, I decided that told it like it was with him.

I asked Joe if he had been married before and he said, "Yes, Mr. Wilson, I've been married three times."

When I asked him how long it had been since he had been divorced he said he had never been divorced. Married three times, but never divorced. This was fairly typical, I found as I grew up.

Joe's wife came back to him as suddenly as she had left and he quickly responded by being his old, cheerful self. He and Mary were the best cotton pickers in the area. Joe claimed he was the best in the county, and I think he was.

Each week, they earned from $40 to $50 picking cotton and this was lots of money at the time, much more than I ever got my hands on. On Saturday night they went to town as did most other blacks. Mary wore old work shoes while walking along the dusty road but she always had her "dress up shoes" in a paper bag. When she arrived in town she changed shoes, then changed again when she walked home with Joe early on Sunday morning.

Some Sunday mornings I would hear a scratching sound on my window screen about daybreak. It was Joe attracting my attention.

"Mr. Wilson, Mr. Wilson, wake up, I need to talk to you," he whispered.

He was afraid my dad would hear him.

"Mr. Wilson, I spent all my money last night and don't have any money to smoke on this week. If you will lend me 25¢, I'll pay you back 30¢ come Saturday."

I always did this and he could buy five sacks of Bull Durham smoking tobacco with the quarter. He always paid me on time. He didn't have to worry about food as he and his wife ate in our kitchen at a separate table. This was a part of their arrangement due to his wife helping my mother a few hours each day. They ate at their table at the end of the kitchen and we at ours. Papa and Joe talked across the intervening space about work schedules and what needed to be done. Joe and Mary were almost like family members, but they kept their distance and never broke those unwritten rules about how they might enter the house or address family members. To write this makes me feel ashamed and one who reads it in today's world may even get angry, but that's the way it was. We had absolutely no feeling that we were discriminating against Joe and Mary.

Once I broke the rules pretty badly, in an innocent manner. We had gotten behind in our field work because of too much rain, and weeds were about to take over our cotton fields. So my father hired a crew from Moorhead to come out to help. These were day hands who didn't live on any farm. Generally, they were not as good workers as those who lived and worked on farms as sharecroppers.

This particular crew was headed up by a Mr. Anderson, a black day worker who was also a preacher. He enjoyed great local renown as a cotton chopper. We didn't know how good he was, but Joe McMillan, about 35 years of age, immediately challenged Mr. Anderson to see who was best. Hubert was still at home that summer and was supervising the whole crew including me. There were about twenty in all. My father didn't approve of hired workers leaning on their hoe handles and loafing, but he also disliked people doing a sloppy job of cutting out too many cotton plants and leaving too many weeds.

The workers began complaining because Hubert wouldn't let Joe and Mr. Anderson settle the question as to who was best. So finally he gave in and set up the rules. I know he thought Papa was in some distant part of the farm and wouldn't know about the hoeing contest.

Joe and Mr. Anderson were to start at the ends of two side-by-side rows and the one finishing first was to be the champion. When they started there was cheering for each, but more for Mr. Anderson than for Joe because most of the workers were from town.

When they were about half way down the row I heard Joe say, "Mr. Anderson, you may beat me but it's because you aren't doing the job right. If Mr. Ferguson sees the kind of work you are doing he will fire you on the spot."

Mr. Anderson didn't pay much attention to what Joe said and began to pull away from Joe. Hubert was cheering for Joe, and for some reason I can't explain, I began pulling for Mr. Anderson.

I was saying, "Come on Mr. Anderson! Come on Mr. Anderson! Beat him, Mr. Anderson!"

Anderson did win, beating Joe about ten feet.

Just at that time Papa came out of the nearby woods and saw what was going on. He walked up and down the rows Joe and Mr. Anderson had hoed, inspecting the quality of work they had done. Everyone was as quiet as a mouse.

He then walked back to the end of the row and said, "Anderson, I'll pay you off at the end of the day and you are fired."

It seemed that Joe knew what Anderson should expect. Later, I found that Papa had been watching the quality of work Mr. Anderson was doing and the hoeing race was the straw that broke the camel's back.

On the way home from the field, Hubert said, "Boy, you've got yourself into a peck of trouble. You were calling Anderson "Mr. Anderson" and you know that just isn't done. Don't forget all the other Negroes heard you, too."

I hadn't given it any thought during the excitement of the race, but now I knew it was a mistake. Papa never said a word to me about the incident. It may be he was too far away at the time to hear what I was saying, but most probably he didn't really care how I addressed Mr. Anderson.

In those days blacks didn't want to be called black. "Black is Beautiful" had never been heard of. In our family blacks were referred to as Negroes and the blacks approved being called Negro. Never, never, did we ever refer to one as "nigger."

Those were strange customs and in later years it became so clear that those customs, in many cases, were demeaning. But we were innocent of purposely hurting the blacks. Two events serve to indicate how ingrained some of those customs and habits were: I shook hands with a black man for the first time when I was in college. He was the college janitor of whom all of us white boys (there were no blacks in college in the South at that time) really thought a great deal. In the other event I rode a very crowded train in the early days of World War II and shared a seat with a black woman and her little girl. It was a new experience for me. If there had been a vacant seat no doubt I would have sat in it. Sitting with the black woman was of such importance in relation to how I was brought up that I remember it to this very day, yet I was talking to them as equals before we had completed our journey. When they left the train in Emporia, Kansas, I helped the lady with her over-head luggage. People are such strange animals, and racism is such an insidious thing.

Chapter 13

GRANDPA

It is pretty hard to believe, but true, that we lived only 250 miles from my father's parents, and yet we had not been back to Alabama between the time I was three and thirteen. Ten years had elapsed, and I couldn't remember Grandpa at all. A decade had gone by since the moonshiners had given my father an ultimatum that he must leave the state, unless he wanted someone else to raise his four kids. Now, 250 miles is only half a day's drive, but back when a high speed was 40 m.p.h. (and that, unsafe, I might add), and the roads nothing much more than wide trails covered with sand or gravel, with mudholes not too uncommon, a 250 mile trip was a trip of a lifetime.

Hubert and I had always wanted to visit Grandpa, maybe more than the other kids, because we had heard so much about his exploits in the Civil War, when he fought on the side of the South, and how he had lived through so many wounds. Hubert was old enough to drive, seventeen or eighteen, I think, and he was to do all the driving, as I was only thirteen at the time. My dad never learned to drive and always seemed to have a son about the right age to do that; later it was daughters. We talked about such a trip all summer, after the flood of 1927 had receded and we had "laid the crops by." It was a hot, dusty summer, but we were anxious and finally persuaded our father to let us all make the trip. We had a T-Model Ford at the time, bought for $550 brand new, and we were proud of it.

Planning a trip in an open car with the necessary luggage, extra cans of gasoline and water, food to eat along the way, and all the other things, as well as six or seven people, was quite a task, but we planned it and set the date. We were to go all the way to Samantha, Alabama, which is thirteen miles north of Tuscaloosa. This was approximately 250 miles, and we planned to do it all in one day, because there were no motels in those days, and our tent was too much to take along.

So, we got up at four a.m., long before daylight, loaded up, checked everything and set out. Our biggest worry was how we might get up Valley Hill. We lived in flat Delta country, and the ring of hills to the east of us was thirty miles away. Those T-Models were good cars in their day, but they didn't have much power to climb any hill, and ours was no exception, being grossly over-loaded in the first place. Valley Hill is the first hill one encounters when driving east from Moorhead. It always seems to be the highest, too. I couldn't even remember ever having seen a hill, nor could the younger kids, either. I guess Valley Hill was probably 600 to 700 feet high, but one reached the top on a meandering road that took maybe two to three miles to get from the bottom to the crest.

Our worries were well founded. Our T-Model just couldn't make it with its load. First, it heated up and steam boiled out of the radiator. That explained why we had extra water, and not just for drinking. After a spell it cooled down, and we decided that all would get out and walk, with each of us carrying some type of luggage or sack; that is, all of us except Hubert, who drove, and Mother, who held one of my young sisters who was too young to walk and climb. The system worked, but we wore ourselves out climbing that hill over a mile or two of rocky gravel road. And, even with its light load, we all had to push at two steep places in the road. After all this time and effort, it was still only about eight in the morning. We stopped at the side of the road under the pine trees, which were new to us kids as they did not grow naturally in the Delta, and ate breakfast. We had no thermos; but Mother had cooked biscuits and sausages for all. We ate biscuit-and-sausage sandwiches, but my memory fails me as to what else, if anything. Anyway, it didn't matter what we ate, as we were so anxious to see and travel through the hill country.

Pretty soon we ran out of water on this hot day and from time to time, we would stop at a farm house in the woods beside the road for fresh water, which almost always was brought up from hand dug wells, three or four feet wide and very deep. The water was always cold and fresh.

With a car loaded so heavily, it was only natural that we would take two extra tires, strapped on the back of the car. Luckily, we needed only one. Just about the time we hit the Alabama state line, one tire went out with a big bang. In those days, you didn't change the whole wheel. You took the wheel off, pried the damaged tire off the rim, and put the good tire on the same rim. We had an air pump to pump up the new tire. It had a plunger on it, which had to be pumped up and down many times before the tire was properly inflated. Without a gauge, it was just guesswork as to when the tire was sufficiently inflated to mount. But finally we mounted it on the wheel, Hubert cranked the engine (with a crank, as it had no self-starter) and we were on our way.

I think I must have slept most of the rest of the trip, as I only remember our arrival. We arrived about six p.m., after fourteen hours of driving; our average speed was about eighteen miles an hour.

What would Grandpa be like? We just couldn't imagine. But we soon found out that at eighty, he was still about six feet tall. What I remember most was his long, flowing, white beard. I still see him, almost like pictures painted of Jesus about 250 years ago, with a prominent forehead and a face covered with a long beard. His eyes were steely blue. He was a minister and farmer and he had traveled over a large area, preaching to groups in the small hill churches, riding his horse all the way.

Right off the bat, Hubert and I wanted him to tell us Civil War stories about the battles he had been in and the wounds he had survived sixty years before. Yet we didn't have nerve enough to ask him anything, until we begged and secured our father's permission.

At last, Hubert got up nerve enough to ask, "Grandpa, will you tell us some of your war stories and show us your wound scar?"

I didn't know it then, but now I understand it wasn't easy for him to talk about the war, the memory of which he hated. You see, my grandfather never owned any slaves in his entire life, and thought slavery was wrong. Still, he was forced by the Confederacy to join the Army. He did believe in States Rights and believed states should have the right to secede from the Union, but, whatever the reason, he found himself in the Army at age nineteen and in action after a short training period. Before he would launch into his war stories and his own experiences, he had to deliver a short lecture to us about how horrible war really is, how wounded scream and die on the battlefield, how much dirt and filth there is, and how frightened a soldier in battle becomes. I guess he knew young boys live in a fantasy world and think war is glamorous and that every soldier, somehow, becomes a hero.

Finally, he took us aside into his bedroom. His house was very large, but it had no electricity or running water. Fresh water came from a deep well in the back yard, that had been hand-dug. His bedroom was just for him and had lots of religious pictures and books on two of the walls.

He started telling us about the battle of Chickamunga, where hand-to-hand fighting occurred. He said that his squad met a squad of bluecoats unexpectedly, and after he fired his muzzle loader and was loading again, an enemy soldier shot him at point blank range, right through the chest. He fell backward into some leaves. He knew he had been shot through the body, but he never lost consciousness. How strange that a large lead bullet could enter and exit his body, and he was still conscious. Then he noticed that if he put his hand over the wound on the front side, he could breathe. So he lay still, surprised that he could breathe normally. Of course, the bullet missed his heart, or he would have been dead. An hour or two later, a medical corpsman came along and examined him, and seeing how badly he was wounded, wondered how he could be breathing so normally. The corpsman moved Grandpa's hand from the wound and he could breath no longer. (The lungs cannot work except in a vacuum, created by the upper thoracic cavity.) He grabbed his hand with his other hand, and again placed it over his chest and again could breath. But, what about the place where the bullet exited his back? He had fallen into dry leaves and, as they were wet from his blood, they began to form an almost airtight cover over the wound in his back. That's how he could breath. As his ribs were broken, both front and back, by the bullet, the corpsman ran a silk handkerchief on a copper wire, through his body, front to back, several times, in order to remove lead fragments (the fragments adhered to the silk). Then they bound him up airtight, so to speak, both front and back, and took him to the aid station, where he made a partial recovery, after which he was sent home to fully recover.

About this time, he took off his shirt, and there was a huge cavity-scar, both on his chest and on his back, with each cavity being almost as big as a fist. To think that he was still living and healthy fifty-eight years later and had reared a huge family, was almost like a believe-it-or-not item, but it was true.

At home, he recovered in record time, and in 1863, volunteered. This time, he was sent to Virginia, where he had a big toe shot off, his arm shot through, and his heel almost shot off. This tale was told so long ago, that all I remember now is that he and his squad (he was a Corporal at the time) were assigned to guard a bridge, and to hold up the enemy until the main part of the retreating army could escape. It was here that he suffered the three wounds, before his group left the bridge on horses hidden in the woods. He didn't like telling that part of his story, as he said he and his squad had deep, secure fox holes and they could pick off the enemy soldiers as they approached the other end of the bridge. He said he knew he killed human beings, and that it still grieved him to think about it. Of course, he, like so many others, grew to regret the horrors of that war, where more American men were killed than were killed in all of our other wars, including the Spanish-American War, World War I, World War II, and up to the middle of the Korean War.

As I looked at the frail eighty-year-old body, I couldn't imagine all the suffering it had endured, and how it had produced such a large family, which I found later was highly respected in that area of Alabama.

I cannot remember a thing that happened on our long trip home, but I vividly remember his stories and what an old, handsome face he had. Forty-eight years later, I visited his tomb, situated on a beautiful hill, surrounded by pine trees beside his country church, near Samantha, Alabama. A large pasture full of fat cattle graced the hill and the valley nearby. Only the day before, I had seen his battle record in the Confederate Records in Montgomery which was the capital of the Confederacy, and now is the capital of Alabama.

To be born again means different things to different people. Nowadays, sophisticated religious theologians have a tendency to be bemused by, and even make a little fun of, people who say they are born again Christians. There were scattered snickers nation-wide when President Carter said he was a born-again Christian. Even the cartoonists had a heyday over that. But the born-again Christians know what he meant and aren't bothered by the amusement enjoyed by others.

A born-again Christian can almost always remember the time and place he openly acknowledged his adherence to Christian principles and resolved to accept Christ as his personal Savior. To do this he had to come down front and be recognized.

We were a Baptist family, with my grandfather having been a Baptist circuit rider, but almost nothing was ever said about Christianity in our home. The family Bible was always nearby

on a table but, except for Mother, who never made any comment, it was read only when there was nothing else to read, as a general rule. The exception was when one of us in school was asked to bring a memorized verse from the Bible to be recited in school chapel or some club meeting. We went to public school and these verses were recited in a group which might include all brands of Protestants as well as Catholics and even a Jew or two. Nobody thought there was anything but good in such a practice in those days. At least, there was no vocal opposition.

In the twenties our Baptist Church held a revival in Moorhead each summer. On such occasions a large tent was rented. It was put up and sawdust was sprinkled liberally on the ground. Electric lights were strung through the tent and some kind of pulpit was placed or built up front. A special effort was made to secure large crowds and there was strong emphasis upon getting the "unsaved" to attend.

An important minister skilled in holding revivals was usually brought in to preach.

I had attended a Pentecostal revival meeting once or twice, and upon going home and telling how they spoke in unknown tongues, and in some cases seemed to have spasms and faint dead away, my parents discouraged my attendance at such meetings.

By this time, age thirteen, I knew most people older than I had been saved. I also began to give it a lot of thought. In 1926 or 1927, one usually thought he would be condemned to hell when he should die, if he had not joined the church and were not a Christian. I had no clear-cut opinion as to what would happen to babies who were not old enough to know anything about Christ and His being the chosen Son of God. I still don't, but trust God to do the right thing.

Anyway, I went to the revival each night from Wednesday to Sunday night and lost so much sleep that I had trouble doing a good job with my hoe when working in the fields by day. I was so sleepy that I could hardly stand up and this didn't make for good work doing the chores, either. All the time, though, I was thinking. Did I want to confess my sins and accept Christ openly? Could I have the nerve to walk down that aisle as others did and take my stand for Christ? I took everything seriously and at the time thought it meant I must never do any evil again. I must always obey my mother and father. I must do things that didn't even seem possible to me at the time. Obeying my mother and father wasn't much of a problem but those dozens of other things one was required to do or not do bothered me.

But on Sunday night, in spite of having the trembles all up and down my body, I went down front when the gathering sang the invitational hymn and the preacher gave his emotional plea.

I don't know exactly what happened to me that night, but whatever it was, was good. I felt a strong sense of relief. I felt that I was at last on some path that led somewhere. I felt that I belonged. That's it; I felt I belonged to Something Greater than I.

From that point on, I felt that my life would be more meaningful. It just seemed as though I was some sort of chosen person. I don't know just why, but I did.

It seemed to me that I had done it myself, that I had made up my own mind, and that I knew what I was doing. As the years passed, my understanding of what I had done grew. I knew that my accepting Christ as my personal Saviour was not going to make a perfect person out of me. I might not even make any changes that could be seen by others. I guess in reality, it meant that I had joined millions of others who have an extra source of strength, who wanted to live better lives, and who pledged to try to know God better over the rest of the days of their lives. I guessed it was up to me to try to make the world a little better place to live.

To be born again is a chilling and thrilling experience, but as I grew older I found that there are other ways of becoming a Christian. Untold millions believe that on a Friday afternoon around 30 A.D. when Christ gasped his last breath on the cross, all mankind were born again, in that God had made it possible for all of us to be Christians and to be members of His Kingdom. Each church denomination has its own theory as to the method of accepting the invitation, but mine was to be born again as in Jesus' quotation that goes something like this, "If ye wish to belong to my Kingdom ye must be born again. . . . ."

Chapter 14

HAWKS AND CHICKENS

As Hubert and I leaned on our hoes while taking a short rest from the back-breaking job of hoeing cotton, we watched a giant-sized chicken hawk glide above our heads on his way from a distant marsh to his nest located high up in a huge oak tree at the east side of the cotton field where we were supposed to be working. As he came nearer and nearer and lower and lower, we could see a two-foot-long snake in his talons. The snake was dead and hanging limply from the clutch of the hawk's bonelike talons, which are almost as sharp as needles. He wheeled in a half circle to avoid some branches, and with a sudden back-peddling of wings, settled gently upon his nest. He was feeding his young.

We had seen this go on for days. Sometimes it was a fish in his talons; other times, frogs. Each time the hawk landed on the nest, we could see two little heads poked up from the nest demanding to be fed.

Each day this happened we got more and more curious as to what little hawks looked like and what the nest was like on the inside. This nest was about seventy feet above the ground and far out on a limb for protection from chicken snakes. These snakes raided bird nests by crawling up the tree trunks and swallowing eggs found in the nest. They did this in chicken nests also, if a chicken made the mistake of building a nest in weeds on the ground. Chicken snakes could swallow eggs much larger than their heads because nature gave them the gift of being able to dislocate their jaws when swallowing a large object. We had seen chicken snakes with as many as three large lumps in their bodies, each lump being an undigested egg larger than the snake's head.

One night at supper, Hubert said he wanted to climb the tree and see what was in the nest. My father said that wouldn't be such a good idea as it would be too dangerous.

"In the first place, that is too high to climb even if you could, and in the second place those hawks would make mincemeat out of your head and arms if they caught you up there bothering their nest. If you tried to protect yourself with your hands you would lose your grip on the branches and fall to the ground like a rock," he added.

Hubert didn't reply and I found out a few days later that he didn't accept what Papa had said as absolutely forbidding him to climb the tree. As for me, I thought Papa had made his point pretty clear, but I could have been wrong.

Soon after this suppertime conversation, we were hoeing together in the same field and the day was hot and humid. About ten we got tired, laid our hoes down and went to the shade of this huge hawk-nest tree. We sat down and fanned ourselves with our sombrero-like straw hats we wore for protection from the hot sun.

After a few minutes, Hubert startled me by saying, "I've just got to see what that nest looks like. We haven't seen any hawks this morning, so they aren't around and won't attack me."

"But how are you going to climb this tree? The trunk is too large to grip and limbs too far apart on the trunk for you to reach from one limb to the next above," I asked.

"You just watch me," he said, "I'm going out to the end of the limbs which hang near the ground and climb the end of the limbs one after the other, until I get up to that nest. As I get higher, the limbs get closer together at the base of the limbs and I can then climb near the trunk. When I get to the limb the nest is on, I will crawl out on it as I would crawl on a log over water. When I get there at least I'll know the color of hawk egg shells. If there are any little hawks in the nest I'll leave them alone and hurry down as I will know the parent hawks will be back to feed their young at any time."

I could see that Hubert had spent lots of time thinking about climbing the tree and the possible perils of the returning adult hawks. With this assurance I felt a little more at ease. But no matter what he might find seventy feet up I wouldn't be able to see for myself. Still, there was no question that Hubert had to be the one to do the climbing, if anyone were to do it, as he was almost five years older than I.

He started up by grasping the end of one of the limbs about thirty-five feet from the trunk of the tree. I boosted him up to the first limb but then he was on his own and all I could do was hope for the best. He worked his way up from one limb to the next, going up and up, but his progress got slower and slower as he climbed. At least, that is the way it seemed to me. Once or twice his feet slipped and he lodged with a jolt astraddle the limb below, but each time he slowly grasped the limb above until he was at the base of the long limb that held the hawk nest.

As he had planned, he began crawling snake-like out the long limb that held the nest. As he worked his way slowly out, I could just imagine him losing his balance and falling off the limb. But after a while he reached the small branches upon which the nest was built. He was so high that he even looked small to me as I watched breathlessly from the ground below.

"What do you see?" I yelled from the ground below.

"You wouldn't believe it," he said. "Boy, this is really something. There are frog skeletons, fish skeletons, and even snake skeletons. I think I see a rat skeleton, too. And say, there are some egg shells, but there is one egg that didn't hatch. It isn't even broken at all."

"Put it in your pocket and bring it down for me to see," I pleaded with him.

"Not on your life," he said. "It would surely break against one of those limbs as I climb down and I can't hold it in one hand as I must use both hands while climbing down."

"Well, you could throw it down and I could catch it," I yelled up at him.

"Yes, and have it smash into a thousand pieces when it hits your hand. But say, you might be able to catch it without it breaking if you will just let your hands give a little bit in the direction the egg is falling when it reaches your hands. You know, just as you do a baseball when you don't want it to sting your hands when you catch it. Just be sure to let your hands give a little. Stand way out from the tree and I will throw it out past the limbs," he instructed me.

So I moved out about twenty feet until I could see him more clearly. After being sure the egg would not hit a limb, he pitched it out. It fell in an arc at first then straight down at about 125 miles an hour, it seemed to me. Just in time, I got my hands under its path. Sure, I let my hands give as it hit, but certainly not fast enough. The egg smashed into a hundred pieces of shell and its contents splashed all over my head, my face, and ran down the bib of my overalls almost to my feet. It was a terrible mess, if I ever saw one.

Have you ever smelled a rotten egg? Have you ever smelled a stink bomb? Their odors are all one and the same, the vilest odor one can ever smell. I should say that it stinks like nothing else and it stays with whatever it touches as badly as skunk odor. That's the way I smelled when Hubert finally made his way slowly down to the ground.

When he came near me he suddenly grabbed his nose and pretended to gag. Maybe it wasn't pretense on his part, but then he began to laugh.

He laughed and laughed at me and said, "I never saw such a smelly mess in my life. I wish I had a picture of you but the picture would not tell how much you stink." He was having a great time as a result of my misery.

Suddenly he quit laughing when I asked, "Now what do we do about me? You know I'll stink up the whole house when we got home and you know Mother will know about it and tell Papa."

Hubert thought a minute and said, "We'll just have to go to that sinkhole in the woods where you can take your clothes off and wash them in the swamp water. Swamp water doesn't smell half as badly as you do. Then your clothes will dry as we walk home."

The idea didn't seem very appealing to me, but it seemed to be the only way out of a bad situation.

We headed for the sinkhole about half a mile away. Hubert wouldn't walk behind me because he said I smelled too "bad." He wanted to lead the way and that's the way we went.

This sinkhole in the woods held water all the year even in the driest years. True, it became stale, but it was the place all the birds and animals in the wood went for their dawn and dusk drinks of water. Their tracks could be seen all around the pond. As we were there near mid-day, there were no animals or birds to be seen. Still, I had the feeling we were being watched by lots of animal and bird eyes in the bushes and trees around the pond.

I took off my smelly clothes, waded into the dank, stale, murky water and sloshed my clothes up and down for quite a while, then tried to wash myself. The truth is I didn't worry about whether I was clean or not, it was my clothing I didn't want to smell so badly. Some soap surely would have helped but we had none.

Upon leaving I wondered, "Will the animals and birds think someone had tried to poison them? Surely, the water tasted differently."

My clothes dried rapidly in the hot sun as we walked home and were bone dry when we entered the back kitchen door. Mother was busy as usual around the kitchen stove and hardly paid any attention to our entrance. By this time, I was somewhat used to the rotten egg odor, but would Mother notice? When one eats onions everyone can smell onion on his breath except the person who ate them. Could it possibly be that way with rotten eggs? Could everyone else smell me except myself? I certainly hoped that wasn't the way it was.

We walked rapidly through the kitchen and past the long kitchen table that would seat twelve people. As we neared the far end of the kitchen I peeped over my shoulder to see if Mother noticed anything out of the ordinary. She had turned toward me and was sniffing the air as she sometimes did when she was cooking something with special odors. But this time her face had a quizzical look on it.

The jig is up, I thought, when she said, "Wilson, you smell like rotten eggs. What have you boys been up to?"

We just casually omitted any real answer by saying something about a bird egg we had found that was spoiled. Of course, we would have told her the truth if she had been any more specific about her question. At least, that is the way we explained it many years later.

For years afterward, Hubert always told that story at family gatherings, and I was always the butt of the story. Still, it gave him so much pleasure in the telling that I did not mind at all. As he told it, that tree got higher and higher, the climb got more and more difficult, the hawk egg got bigger and bigger, but try as hard as he might, he could never make the odor of that rotten egg any worse than it really was.

There were lots of chicken hawks near our house on the farm, and most of them stayed hidden in the woods, only darting out from time to time to pluck a small chicken from our chicken yard. Chickens roamed free and would venture two or three hundred yards from their chicken house. We always had lots of them in the spring, and had some good Sunday chicken dinners. At times, we began to miss chickens and then we could go into the woods and find feathers at the spot where the hawks had their feast. This got bothersome, as they got more and more of our chickens. So, we declared war on them, but nothing seemed to work. Sometimes we could bring a hawk down with a shotgun, but our best luck came from using a high-powered rifle.

I can't remember why I was not out in the cotton fields working that day, but maybe I was running a fever or something. Anyway, I was lying on a bed in our back bedroom, which was almost a lean-to bedroom, large enough for two double beds and a cot. We boys slept there. The ceiling did not really have a dropped ceiling. The ceiling was the roof itself, with exposed rafters, and over the sheathing, a wood shingle roof. As there was no false ceiling, we could always hear the very first drops of rain fall when a storm approached.

About ten that morning, suddenly the chickens began to get very noisy and Mother, who was in the kitchen, yelled, "A hawk is after the chickens. Get your daddy's gun and try to shoot him."

I grabbed the ten-gauge gun. It was a Winchester and had a lever action, just like the .38 Winchester rifles used in the old cowboy movies. But it was a shotgun and not a rifle. The hammer was a receding one, and did not stick up like the hammers on the rifles. This meant it was difficult to let the hammer down, after it had been cocked. If the hammer was let down too suddenly the gun would fire.

I grabbed the gun, which was always standing in a corner waiting for an emergency, and hastily pumped a shell into the firing chamber, all the while heading for the rear door and the chicken yard.

It was too late. The hawk, with a small chicken in his talons, was already about fifty yards away. Before I could draw a bead on him and fire, I knew he was too far away for the shot to be effective. So there was nothing to do but accept defeat by the hawk and return the gun to its position in the corner. But first, I had to let the hammer down slowly. While holding the gun barrel straight up, I tried to gently let the hammer down as I also pulled on the trigger. This was the proper method, but alas, it didn't work out that way. The hammer slipped (I always said my fingers were damp with perspiration) and the gun went off, straight into the roof overhead. Shingles scattered everywhere and there was daylight showing through. I could see a large area of blue sky through the hole that the blast of the shot had made. It had blown a number of shingles off the roof and into splinters.

Of course, the noise was loud and scary inside the house and Mother called from the kitchen, "Are you all right, Wilson?"

I replied, "Yes, I just shot a huge hole through the roof."

She then said, "Well, I guess you had better get Hubert to help you replace the shingles when he gets home."

Mother didn't even come into the room to size up the situation. So many unexpected things happened around the farm that she couldn't allow herself to be upset unless the circumstances were dire indeed. As for the shingles, we always had plenty of them available; my father split the shingles for our roof out of cypress blocks by using his own adz.

I guess it isn't every day that a fourteen-year-old boy shoots part of the roof off his home, but it's a wonder it didn't happen more often than it did, considering the number of guns kept around the house for hunting.

We always had the famous ten-gauge Winchester shotgun I attempted to use on the hawk, but in addition, we had a twelve-gauge pump-gun, a double barrel shotgun, a twelve-gauge single-shot shotgun, a .22 caliber rifle, and a .38 caliber Winchester rifle. Each was used for its own purpose: hunting rabbits, squirrels, and quail. The rifles were used mostly for stationary targets, like a hawk sitting high on a limb of a tree. Having these guns didn't mean we wanted to start our private war, but it did mean they had to be cleaned at fairly regular intervals to avoid rust.

One night, while sitting around the fire in the fall of the year, we were cleaning our guns after a rabbit hunt in the afternoon. Clara, my oldest sister, had come home from Jackson, where she was working, and had hunted with us. Clara didn't care all that much about hunting or cleaning guns, but she was cleaning the double barrel shotgun. It had a safety but no hammer.

After cleaning it she decided to check its action to see if everything worked properly before putting it away in a corner. She was loading it, breaking it down, emptying its chamber, loading it again, closing its breach and putting it through normal tests. While doing this she kept the barrel pointed at the ceiling or toward the wall on her left.

Something went wrong. For some reason neither she nor we could figure out, she pulled both triggers when the gun was loaded and pointed toward the wall. What a blast!! Both barrels fired at once into the wall behind which was a closet full of clothes. It was the only closet built into the original house plan. A large hole was blown in the wall and the clothes were riddled. We found shot on the closet floor for years afterward. Papa never did repair the hole in the wall. He wanted it to be a reminder of how we must always be careful when cleaning or handling guns.

Hundreds of times in the following years visitors would ask, "What made that hole in your wall, Mr. Ferguson?"

Papa would always tell how it happened. I'm just thankful Clara was almost never home to have to hear the questions answered.

On another occasion, when were were at home, with all of us on beds for our noon rest which followed lunch, I was napping lightly when there was a blast just above my head. Splinters showered all around me. My brother Louis was playing with the .22 rifle in the room on the other side of the wall and had accidentally fired the gun. I yelled at him to please be careful as he had almost shot me. He said that he would and the incident was closed. The bullet hole was there the last time I saw the house; just another reminder.

For years, we tried to get Mr. J. S. Vandiver, the superintendent of the school system, to go hunting with us. He said he wanted to do this but always seemed busy on the Saturdays when we usually hunted.

One Saturday, he was free and we planned a combination quail and rabbit hunt. There were about eight of us and we used no dogs. We lined up and walked through the woods and briar patches with the intention of shooting at any quail or rabbit that might take off flying or running in front of us.

We had hunted only a short time when we detected some quail in a briar patch. They were hiding in dead leaves. After surrounding the small area of vines and briars, Louis was to walk into the vines and flush the quail. On such occasions everyone knew he was to shoot high, over the heads of the other hunters.

When the quail flushed straight upward and then outward, each one of us took a shot at a quail. One or two fell, but there were more misses than hits. My uncle said Mr. Vandiver got his bird, but my uncle didn't know at the time that he got me. One of his shot had hit a small limb of a sapling and ricocheted off toward me. It went through my upper lip just under my nose and lodged harmlessly against an upper tooth. I spit the shot and a mess of blood out and didn't really feel all that badly hurt.

Mr. Vandiver was on the opposite side of the briar patch but my father was nearby.

When I told him about the shot and he had examined me, he said, "You know Mr. Vandiver is just a little bit gunshy, and if he knows you are shot he will want to quit the hunt right now. Just go home and put some iodine on it, and except for some swelling you will be okay."

He said he would tell Mr. Vandiver that I got sick at my stomach and had to go home.

I surely did hate to miss that hunt with Mr. Vandiver, but I did as instructed, and when they gathered in the front yard after the hunt I watched them as they unloaded their guns and talked about all the game they brought home. Mr. Vandiver never did know that I had been shot. A few years later he was elected Mississippi State Superintendent of Education. In that job he could do more good for the schools than he could do as superintendent of Sunflower Agricultural High School in Moorhead.

Clara, my oldest sister, came home at times from her job in Jackson. She came home mostly to rest but soon got bored and then began to look around for things to do.

During the years she was coming home while most of the younger kids were still at home, we raised chickens to eat, but we also raised guineas and turkeys mostly as a hobby, something for the kids to look after.

Of course, the chicken nests were in the chicken house, but guineas and turkeys were wily creatures, always seeking secrecy as to where they were making their nests and laying their eggs. We never ate guinea or turkey eggs as we always heard they were too strong and not all that good for human consumption. I'm surprised to this day that we didn't try them out to see for ourselves, but we didn't.

We knew the turkeys were nesting somewhere but couldn't find their nests. About laying time, we thought about eleven in the morning, one of us would watch the turkeys carefully to see if one of the hen turkeys disappeared suddenly. We could never find the nest this way. The turkey just ducked into some vines and disappeared. All we knew was that the nests had to be in some of the vines that grew profusely along the railroad embankment in front of our house. Some of these vines had thorns on them and some didn't. The blackberry vines were sticker-bearing for certain.

On one of the occasions when Clara came home for a short vacation we were in the annual process of hunting for the guinea and turkey nests, but it was the latter in which we were most interested. Clara, probably bored by this time with nothing to do on the farm, volunteered to find the turkey nest before her week at home ended. She began watching and each day saw a hen turkey look all around with head extended high to see if the coast were clear, and then suddenly disappear.

About four p.m. on a day when one of the turkeys had gone through this ritual, Clara went to the spot of disappearance and noted a very narrow, almost tube-like hole through the vines. By easing quietly along and looking carefully she finally found the nest, but she found much more than a turkey nest.

A huge chicken snake, a non-poisonous, non-biting snake, noted for robbing chicken nests of eggs, was right in the middle of the nest and had already swallowed two eggs. One was already about half way down its body, one had just entered its stomach, and with jaws dislocated for swallowing, it had a third turkey egg in its mouth; Clara yelled at the top of her voice for someone to quickly bring her a hoe. Kathleen, a younger sister, obliged.

Clara's plan was to chop down hard on the snake and kill him. All snakes were evil, to her way of thinking, and this chicken snake, which ate lots of bugs, insects, and mice, was no exception. With the hoe in her hands she took aim at the snake, which could hardly move with two huge turkey eggs already swallowed and one in its extended mouth. With a mighty swing she drew the hoe up over her head and then struck quickly, as hard as she could. The vines killed the force of the blow and it didn't hurt the snake. She saw that due to the vine cover there was no way she could kill the snake with the hoe.

She then yelled, "I'll pin the snake down with the hoe and then someone please get an ax. It will cut through the vines."

I don't recall who, but someone ran to the house for an ax as Sister placed the hoe on the snake's neck and began to press downward as hard as she could. But this snake was large and strong and began to slide out from under the hoe blade. Sister became frantic and pressed down still harder. Suddenly, the hoe handle broke from the extra pressure she had exerted and Sister fell into the vines directly on top of the snake and turkey nest.

Such yelling and hollering I don't think I have ever heard out of a woman, but it was really no wonder. To fall on top of a huge chicken snake in sticker-filled vines is no fun under any circumstances. No one could get to her quickly and during the constant yelling and crying, the snake escaped. When someone did get to her and the nest the snake was nowhere to be seen. He escaped, no doubt to raid other nests in the future. As for Sister, her feelings were hurt and she had scratches on her hands and arms.

This was a family story for years and every time it was told in Clara's presence she just smiled and said nothing. I always thought she must have felt as badly as I did when the rotten hawk egg splattered down my face and clothes.

Chapter 15

THE GREAT MULE RACE

When we were kids, fruit, especially fresh fruit of any kind, was a real treat and we got very little of it, due to its expense and there being so many of us. Dried fruit, apples and apricots, we got quite often, and Mother made pies of it. But this, too, was a special treat, which we got only on Sundays or birthdays.

For one type of dessert, we depended largely upon blackberries, which grew wild in the woods and along fence rows on the farms. We always spotted the good-looking blackberries before they ripened, so we would know where to go before anybody else picked them, and when they were ripe, all of us, young and old, took buckets and washtubs to the blackberry patches and picked them by the gallons. When finished, all of us had dozens of blackberry "stickers" in our hands, but they were ignored. Mother canned the blackberries and in winter made blackberry pie. We also placed blackberries in bowls, poured milk over them, and with the addition of meager amounts of sugar, which was pretty expensive, ate them. They were good this way, but after so long a time of eating the same dessert, it gets pretty old and tasteless.

The same goes for boiled eggs. I had a boiled egg and a biscuit and sausage, or a biscuit and pork of some kind, for lunch in my school lunch bucket almost every day. And can you believe this? A boy named G. C. Scroggins, whose dad had a small grocery store, had an apple in his lunch box almost every day of the world.

He got tired of apples and one day said, "Wilson, would you trade that boiled egg for my apple?"

Boy, I knew a good thing when I saw it, but acted a little reluctant.

"Oh, I don't know," I said, "That apple is pretty small and this is a Leghorn egg and you know how big they are."

"Aw, come on, Wilson, you know my apple is worth every bit as much as one boiled egg."

So I said, "Okay."

And we traded. I don't know how many times we traded after that, but that lucky G. C. had much tastier things for lunch than I did. But do you think I would have let him know? Not on your life.

And that brings me to the banana part of my story. Ware's Grocery Store always seemed to have plenty of rock candy in their glass enclosed cases and, of course, that was off limits to us kids, because of the expense. This isn't to say we didn't ever get candy to eat, because we did, but on those occasions it was a real treat. Behind the counter, Mr. Ware always had his dried apples and cracker barrels, but he also had a real delicacy hanging from the ceiling—bananas. Those bananas always looked so good to Hubert and me when we drove the wagon to town for our week's supply of groceries on Saturday.

Hubert and I always imagined that the best thing that could happen to us would be to get all the bananas we could eat, just one time in our lives. Mother did try to make a banana cake on my birthday. I was the only kid she did this for, but she did other things for the other kids. It was just that she knew that I liked bananas in any form.

One day, a Friday I think it was, Hubert and I got to talking about what we liked to eat and suddenly he said something I had always thought.

"You know, I just wish that I could get all the bananas I want to eat someday."

I don't think he knew it, but he was voicing my secret thought.

The next day, we were to drive the wagon over that rough gravel road to town for our week's supply of groceries, and for the Negro families on the farm, also. I don't know exactly where we had gotten the money, but we had about a dollar and a half saved up, maybe from hiring out to hoe cotton for the farmer down the road. It was all ours, with no strings attached, so we decided that after we had our grocery order filled and loaded into the wagon, we would then spend the dollar and a half for bananas. The wagon was almost full of groceries for four families for about a week, and then we went in to make our purchase.

In those days, bananas were very cheap. We got three dozen bananas and had some change coming back.

Mr. Ware, the groceryman, said, "Your mother must plan on a few banana cakes for your family. This is more than you usually get."

"Yes," Hubert, our spokesman, said. "She'll make a few cakes."

The truth is, I never knew her to make more than one at a time, but I kept quiet.

We took the huge sack of bananas out to the wagon, mounted the spring-supported seat, and headed out of town. It took lots of restraint on our part to delay until we were out of town. My Aunt Inez lived near the edge of town and we knew we would have to wait until we were past her house, as she might see us and tell on us, reporting to our parents that were were eating bananas as we passed her house. We loved Aunt Inez very much because of the good things she sometimes invited us in to eat, but we also knew she was a tattletale. She was one of the first in town to get a phone and she used it almost every waking hour, calling all others who had phones. As a result, my father, although he was civil to her, said she was a gossip. We had no phone, but he heard those phone-talk reports from others and, most likely, they were true. Aunt Inez could tell you just about anything that was going on in town, good or bad.

It seemed such a long time, when in reality it was only about ten minutes, before we had safely passed Aunt Inez's house. We had proof Aunt Inez was a tattler because of what Hubert and I called "The Great Mule Race."

We rode Old George to school some years before. George was not only smart, he was also the fastest mule around. A boy named Jack Thomas rode a large gray mule to school by himself, while we rode Old George double, Hubert in the saddle and me behind on a blanket, holding on to Hubert's waist. Jack began to brag around school that his mule was the fastest there was around Moorhead. I always thought he said it for our benefit, but whether he did or not, I'll never know. Anyway, Hubert, being older than I, just couldn't have our Old George put down like that and said he would bet a quarter that George, with us on his back, could outrun Jack out to the city limits, which was about half-mile away from the front of the school. Aunt Inez's house was less than half a mile away, so that meant we would have to race past her house, but we didn't think about that. Of course, all the kids were hanging around and heard Jack bragging, as well as the challenge. Everyone knows how most boys are. They just can't take dares if they have a chance to win or it is made in front of classmates. So we agreed on the race.

Being quite a bit younger and more timid than Hubert, I began to get cold feet about the race and I pulled him aside, out of earshot of the others. "Hubert, let's don't race Jack and his mule. You know Papa has a rule about racing our work mules. He says it's not being fair to them. Besides, Jack's mule just grazes in his pasture all day long and doesn't have to pull a plow from sun-up to sun-down like Old George does. Let's don't do it, or if you do, I'll walk, because two of us will overload Old George and give Jack and his mule an advantage."

Hubert seemed so confident and I couldn't understand why, until he said, "Jack's mule may start out fast, but he's so much like a quarter horse, that he can't run more that a quarter of a mile at full speed. He'll tire out, but remember Old George has plenty of stamina from pulling a plow all day long. He'll start out slow, but he'll finish faster. Also, he is used to carrying both of us, so don't worry about the weight."

All of this made pretty fair sense to me, so I said, "Okay."

By this time, there were maybe twenty or twenty-five kids around, even some of the girls, and they began clamoring for us to let them walk down the road a ways so they could see us race better than just from the line from which we were to start. So we waited awhile for them to walk about 200 or 300 yards. What we forgot was that the kids took their viewing position almost in front of Aunt Inez's house. She never said, but I always believed she probably heard them outside on the road and went out on her front porch to watch, or at least see what all the commotion was about.

Back on the starting line, we got everything tied down the best we could—books in their straps and raincoats tied up securely. I took a tight grip on Hubert's waist. Jack was so unconcerned all the while that you would have thought he was a professional jockey. He said he would let Hubert count three for the start. Jack's gray mule pranced around nervously before the start, but Old George just stood there taking everything in very calmly and attempted to go to the side of the road and eat a clump of grass. Hubert reigned him back and counted to three.

Off we went, and the start was just like Hubert had predicted. Jack and his gray took off like a jackrabbit and got a quick lead. I held on for dear life, as Old George took a steady gallop. He didn't seem very interested in the race in the beginning. We didn't dare kick him in the flanks, as he would have immediately stopped and started bucking. Hubert could only urge him on with kind words and gentle pats on his front shoulders.

After about one hundred fifty yards Jack turned around and made fun of us, as his gray was cruising along about twenty yards in front. Soon we passed the group of kids who had walked down the road to watch the race. As we passed, they yelled for us, as kids seem to always favor the underdog. I guess it was then that Old George began to take an interest in things. I could feel his muscles tighten under me and he picked up the pace. Hubert didn't urge him on too much; he knew a half mile is a long way.

As we passed the group of kids, we also passed Aunt Inez's house beside the road. And wouldn't you just know it would happen? She was on the front porch and saw us as we passed by, coats and books flapping in the breeze we were creating.

I yelled at Hubert, "Aunt Inez saw us as we passed her house."

He said, "It's too late now, the fat's in the fire. I've got to win this race and Jack's quarter."

Little by little, we gained, and then, after the quarter mile mark, the picture really began to change.

I was no mule racing expert, but even my untrained eye told me that Jack's gray was tiring. Just like Hubert had said, he didn't have any stamina. As he tired, Old George's long hours of pulling a plow paid off for us. He kept up his gallop and seemed to gain strength. I've always said Old George was smarter than any horse or mule I have ever seen. He seemed to know what it was all about and I believe he really got the idea that he was supposed to outrun that gray. Whether that's right or not, I'll never know, but as he kept up his steady stride and strong pace, Jack seemed to become panicky and started to whip the gray across the flanks. But it didn't do any good. The gray was simply worn out. He slowed more and more, and Old George continued to gallop steadily. At the three-eighths mile mark, the race was really over. The gray just slowed down to a walk. He had done his best, but he just wasn't in shape for a half mile race—a quarter mile, yes, but not a half mile. Jack pulled him up and stopped. We turned and rode George back to him. Jack was a good sport and acknowledged he was beaten.

He said, "If I had had any more money, I would have bet you a dollar I could beat you on my gray."

Hubert said, " Well, all I want is a quarter, fork it over."

Jack searched around in his pants and found that he didn't have even a quarter.

He said, "I'll give it to you Monday at school."

The last I knew is that Jack never did pay Hubert, but it wasn't the last I heard of the race.

About a week after, Aunt Inez came down and visited us on our farm. Her husband was Uncle Earl who had fired his pistol to make the man in the car think he had a blowout. After she left, we knew she had spilled the beans, because Papa called Hubert and me out into the back yard to chat. This time, he didn't paddle or switch us, as he probably thought Hubert was really pretty big and it would humiliate him too much. And because Hubert got off, I did too. But that wasn't the end of it.

He just told us that we couldn't hunt for the first week of the hunting season, which was coming up pretty soon after.

After he gave us the penalty, Hubert said, "Boy, I wish he had paddled us. Giving up hunting is worse than a paddling."

So that is how we knew Aunt Inez was a tattletale and that's why we waited until we were past her house to reach for the first banana.

As we rode along on that rough gravel road, Hubert, who was driving, said, "Okay, let's have our banana feast."

I pulled out two bananas, we peeled them and started eating. Oh, boy! They were good! The first ones disappeared almost in nothing flat and so I dug out two more from the large brown paper sack. We both noted that both of us had slowed down noticeably, in the speed with which we ate the second ones. Still, we kept eating.

On the third round, after a couple of bites, I said, "Had you thought about our not having any water to drink to wash the bananas down?"

Of course, he hadn't thought about it and neither had I. Suddenly, we had our fill of bananas and neither of us could even finish the third one. So what could we do now? Mother didn't expect any bananas, as she didn't put them on the long grocery list. Should we hide them in the smokehouse or barn and eat them later? We couldn't hide them in the house, as ripe bananas

have quite a noticeable odor. If we hid them anyplace other than the house, mice or rats would get them.

So we decided to do what seemed the best thing under the circumstances; tell Mother that we had saved our money and bought all of those bananas so she could bake a cake, and also, make the family some banana pudding, which all of us liked.

As I remember it, Hubert did the talking for he could keep a straight face and he knew I couldn't. Mother didn't seem to suspect anything, and thought we had done a good turn, but she found out later. It was a tale we finally told years later, before our parents died. One other thing—Aunt Inez may have tattled on us about the mule race, but she never knew about the bananas.

There is an old joke that says, in effect, that mules are so stubborn and hard-headed that one must first hit them over the head with a two by four plank in order to first get their attention. Well, that just isn't so, for most mules. In some respects, mules are like people, they differ in degrees of stubbornness and in intelligence.

We always had about seven mules for our 160 acre farm. All of them had names and all had differing dispositions. Each one had his own stall in which he was fed in the barn and when the barn doors were opened no mule ever went into another's stall. He wanted his own.

We boys always said Papa thought more of his mules than he did of his boys because he took extra time to be sure they were healthy and fed properly. If one got a sore spot on his shoulder because of a harness rubbing his skin raw, Papa had lots of lotions to apply to the sore spot. Papa had no use for horses for the kind of jobs we needed done. He always said the mule's small hooves (much smaller than horses' hooves) enabled them to work better in the gumbo soil of the Delta. He thought mules were less temperamental than horses and that most of them could be trained easier and better than horses. Mules were indispensable in the days before tractors were adapted to use in cultivating row crops.

Three of our mules stood out above the rest. Dan was strong, muscular, and could run the fastest, but he was built like a 100 yard dash man. Despite all his muscle he seemed to tire more quickly than the others. Tobe was a little mule and so gentle that we didn't mind little kids playing around him. Tobe was docile. He was used for lighter pulling jobs. George was the one we rode to school when the school bus couldn't make it on the muddy country roads. We called him Old George as if he had a two-word name. He was a very special mule.

Old George was more than a mule; he was a character. Sometimes I thought a circus horse trainer could have trained him to do everything except perhaps talk. George could seem to anticipate things. As an example, he would be drowsily looking at the ground as if innocent of all things around him, but he would actually be watching to see if anyone left the corral gate open and unattended. If such a thing happened he would be off like a shot and hard to catch.

When Mother rang the farm bell each day at 11:30 as a signal for everyone to quit working and come home for the lunch hour, Old George would stop in his tracks even in the middle of a row and expect one to unhitch him, climb on his back and ride him to the barn for his water and food. No amount of urging short of beating him would get him to move in any direction except the barn. When he arrived at the barn, someone would be busily pumping water from the pitcher pump into a water tank. If the water in the tank were just a little warm or partially stagnant, George would simply drink out of the U-shaped spout from the pump until he had his fill. The other mules drank out of the tank. Old George wanted his water cold and fresh.

George was a gentle mule to ride and we rode him to school many times over the muddy roads, but we quickly learned that the rider behind the saddle must keep his feet from dangling against George's flanks directly in front of his rear legs. If one did touch his flanks he would buck gently as a signal as to what was happening. If a gentle buck didn't get his message across, he would buck much more violently and rid himself of the rider.

One of George's smartest tricks had to do with the door to the corn crib. Once or twice when entering the barn we would find the corn crib door open and George would be in the middle of the crib, wading in corn up to his stomach and eating his fill of corn on the cob. We would blame each other for having left the corn crib door open. After this happened twice we decided that George was the culprit and spied on him from between the cracks in the planks on the harness room.

The crib door was secured by a wooden latch about two feet long that was lop-sided. The latch was mounted off-center so that when the handle was down there was no way for the door to open from pressure either inside or out. With the handle up, the door was not secured and could be opened with one's fingers or by itself from pressure within. There was almost always some pressure within, from the corn inside. George was seen using his nose to turn the handle of the latch straight up. When this happened the door swung partially open. He then used his nose to push the door fully open. He would climb the two feet into the corn crib and eat to his heart's content. I knew monkeys could be trained to do such things but George is the only mule I ever heard of who did things such as this that seemed to require some thinking ability.

Sometimes one of us would leave the corral gate open and unattended. When this happened George not only ran out, he led all the other mules on a wild chase around the farm. To round them up required the efforts of all of us and some of the Negro tenants.

On one occasion when this happened, we worked for two hours to round them up, get bridles on them, and herd them back to the barn corral. When almost there, George would break out of our encirclement, leading the other mules away again. As they ran through the cotton some of it was destroyed and once, in the fall of the year when cotton was ripe and ready to be picked, they knocked out several hundred pounds of cotton when running on one of their gang escapes. It was always Old George who led them.

Finally, one fall day Papa said he knew how to get the mules back in the corral. He went to the house and loaded his ten-gauge shotgun with 8.5 bird shot with a light powder load. This time, when George led the other mules in a break-out of the encirclement, Papa got a chance to shoot him in the rear end from a distance of about eighty yards. From this distance the shot stung but did not penetrate his skin. He got the message instantly, turned around in his stride with all the others following and ran voluntarily into the corral. There seemed to be no question that he understood the cause of that shotgun blast.

From that time, for many months when the mules got out with George leading them, Papa would get out his gun and just wave it at Old George. When he did this, the chase was over because that mule knew he would be shot enough to hurt.

When Hubert and I rode George to school we put him in a barn belonging to a friend of my father's. He had the freedom of a small corral. We usually brought a sack of corn for him for lunchtime. On one of those days, Buddy Collins, a town boy who was the type who would try 'most anything once, asked Hubert if he could ride George around the corral after we had saddled up to go home from school.

Hubert said, "Buddy, I don't mind, but Old George won't budge out of his tracks if you get on him. He will only go for us."

Buddy didn't believe this and repeated his request to ride George.

Finally, Hubert said, "Okay, but remember I told you he won't go for you."

Buddy mounted the saddle, but the stirrups were a little long for him. Sure enough, George didn't budge when Buddy yelled "Giddyap" or some such word. Nothing would move Old George. Right then Hubert let his tendency to play tricks on people show.

He looked at me and winked and then said, "Buddy, the only way you will get him to go is to kick him in the flanks just in front of his rear legs."

We knew what to expect to happen and it did. George started bucking and although Buddy tried to hold on the saddle horn for dear life, he didn't stay mounted for long. After landing on his front feet very hard, George's whole body seemed to explode upward in one mighty leap. Buddy was no professional rider and he flew upward about four feet and sideways about six feet, then fell into a pile of manure. Of course, all the kids who were watching laughed and jeered Buddy something awful. Hubert acted so contrite. He went into the barn and got the gunny sack in which we had brought George's corn and began trying to rub the manure off Buddy.

I heard him say, and he said it with a straight face, "Buddy, I wonder what got into that crazy mule. Just to think a mule as gentle as Old George would do such a thing like that sure is a shock to me."

Buddy thought he was sincere and said, "I don't know either, but I don't want on that mule's back again."

George lived to be twenty years old and for the last few years of his life we took special care of him, letting him do little work, but feeding him well. We always like to run our hands over his nose because it felt like velvet, and to have him rub his nose against our cheeks. We petted him more than we did any other mule, but old age finally did him in. That was one time all of us kids, older ones as well as younger ones, cried.

Chapter 16

GROWING UP

The news in the *Commercial Appeal* didn't appeal to me all that much, but the sports, especially the baseball news, did. I read box scores and ratings so much that I could give the batting averages of Babe Ruth, Lou Gehrig and many other stars of the late 'twenties. Some of my brothers and sisters thought I was crazy to be so hung up on baseball when all I had to play with up, until the seventh grade, was baseballs made of string saved from grocery packages, wound as tightly as possible and then stitched with a needle and thread. There was no cover for these balls. My father didn't seem to mind my rather singular interest in baseball. Or if he did, he didn't say anything. Gabby Harnett was the big man among the catchers in those days. He played for the Chicago Cubs.

So, I decided to be a big league catcher on a par with Gabby Harnett, no less. That year, I think my eighth-grade year, my father allowed me and Hubert to sharecrop seven acres of cotton. This was a big venture, as we were to do all the other work on the farm we were supposed to do.

No doubt we put in a little extra effort and fertilizer on our seven acres and it produced more than any other land in cotton that year. Papa made good, gave us the money, and said we could spend it any way we wanted as long as it was something we needed. I not only knew what I wanted, but it was something I needed, in my opinion. So I ordered a complete catcher's outfit; a mask, chest protector, shin guards, and catcher's mitt. It was a left-handed mitt as I am left handed. I played in tennis shoes. I was the only eighth-grade catcher in our county with a complete catcher's outfit.

Behind the plate I was pretty good, as the batters swinging, striking out, or tipping the ball didn't bother me at all. But an uncle told me there had never been a major league catcher who was left handed. That did it. I knew right then that this was the wrong position for me. He said that there were many left-handed first basemen in the majors. That also did it. I knew instantly that I was to be a first baseman. So I sold my catcher's outfit, or traded it to someone, and got a first baseman's mitt by Sears Roebuck mail order catalogue. This led to the finest present I had ever had in my life, and this is the way it came about.

Hubert was already out of high school when I was in ninth grade at Sunflower Agriculture High School. He was working for a meat packing and distribution company and delivering meat over a sixty-mile area, quite a distance in those days. In high school, Hubert didn't care a great deal for baseball as he was interested mostly in girls, and only interested in making passing grades so he could get out and go to work. According to my memory, he spent more time with the girls than he spent studying and I guess I know why—he seemed to always be going with the prettiest girl in school. Still, it wasn't all that one sided, as Hubert was about 6 ft. 1 in. tall in high school and was pretty good looking, himself. I was different. My love for baseball came first, good grades second, and interest in girls a far distant third, at least until I was about seventeen. As a freshman, I made the team at first base.

I was a spindly 125-pounder about 5 ft. 9 in. tall at the time. I wasn't muscular despite all the hard work and long, boring hours on the farm. And to tell the truth, I also didn't have the best coordination. Just say I was average except in my fielding. As is so often the case even in the major leagues, the best fielder on the team is the poorest hitter, and I was close to it. I could play that first base position with skill and that's the reason I made the team. To anyone who knows about high school baseball, it is common knowledge that the throws to first base are more of the wild sort than of the on-the-target kind. This requires fielding and this I could do.

Our team had uniforms, regular baseball caps, and played in tennis shoes. We were a weak-hitting outfit and almost any of the delta teams could have beaten us except for our catcher, Jack Grantham, and our pitcher, Ralph Welch. Jack was aggressive and could hit almost any pitcher and Welch was tall and rangy and could throw a curve ball that made most high school hitters look silly. Welch had the hitters fanning the air on pitches that were really balls to the worst umpire.

Why I fell for Grantham's line, I don't know, but he told me that to really play baseball one had to be aggressive and to chew tobacco. The first part I could accept, but the chewing tobacco bit didn't quite ring true to me.

Still, I felt that I needed all the help I could get to be a good ball player so one day I said, 'Jack, get me a chew of tobacco and I'll try it."

We were at practice.

The tobacco tasted terrible, but I stuck it out as best I could, spitting out the juice as often as possible so as to get the bad taste out of my mouth.

Later that same day, in our daily practice game, my tobacco chewing came to an abrupt end. I got so excited sliding into home plate, a new experience for me, that I swallowed the cud of tobacco which was between my cheek and jaw. Before you could say, "Jack Robinson," I began to get sick at my stomach. After a few minutes I thought I would just die on the spot while on defense at first base. I didn't let the coach know my trouble. He would have chewed me up and spit me out for sure.

The small stands near first base saved me. As I felt the cud of tobacco coming up I ran behind the stands and luckily vomited the entire cud of tobacco. In just a few seconds I felt much better. I returned to first base but never returned to chewing tobacco. It was a a good lesson quickly learned and without much cost.

Hubert, this brother of mine who was five years older, always seemed to want to look out for me. He wanted me to make the good grades in school that he could have made but didn't, because of so many other interests. He encouraged me to study hard, be active in debate, and write a column for the school newspaper, but most of all he encouraged my good grades. One day he came up with a big surprise.

Early in the fall he told me that if I would made the "excellent list" for the entire year until baseball season started, he would buy me a pair of cleated baseball shoes. What an incentive! Our school had an "excellent list" and an "unsatisfactory list" which was posted on the bulletin board each two weeks. This was not a report card; it was mostly a progress report. Each teacher made up such a list every two weeks. It was understood that I could order the baseball shoes from Sears Roebuck's catalogue put out by the Memphis store.

Of course, we always had the latest copy of the Sears Catalogue and it took me only a minute or two to pick out the shoes I wanted. When I saw that they cost $4.25 my hopes fell, as I doubted Hubert could afford to buy them for me. There was just no way I could earn any money working on our own farm and my dad certainly couldn't help, with others to worry about.

On the next weekend when Hubert came by I told him about the price of the shoes. I also told him they were the cheapest Sears had. He didn't seem to mind. He just repeated his promise but the grades had to be excellent on all my subjects. I've learned in later years all about how kids should learn for learning's sake and that rewards for good grades are bad for character building. Maybe so, but I doubt if any kids worked harder than I did. Sure enough, I made it, but for the last month before March, I waited with bated breath to see my name on the excellent list.

And then the shoes came, and were they a sight to behold! Shiny black leather with metal cleats just like the professionals wore, or at least that's what I thought. Our first big game was scheduled two days later and we didn't get to work out the day before the game because of a rain.

What a game! We were to go to Shaw, about thirty-five miles away, quite a trip in 1930. My brother was to be in the area that day delivering meat and made plans to see the game. Shaw had a great reputation for having a fine baseball team. Fact is, they were known far and wide as a baseball town and had the best team in the Delta and that means from Greenville on the west to Greenwood on the east and from Clarksdale on the north to Vicksburg on the south. They were good!!!

To make matters worse, they had a pitcher such as high school teams seldom have. His name was Red Godbold. Just think of that name; it alone struck fear into the hearts of our young players including me, I'm sorry to say. Everybody said Red wet the balls down and rubbed them in the dirt to discolor them, making them much harder to see than they would have been if they had been clean and white. You see, he was a fast ball pitcher and he hoped to mow us down with speed and a darkened ball we could hardly see anyway.

The game started and I quickly spotted Hubert, my brother, in the stands. He knew Red Godbold's reputation and knew we were underdogs. To this day I remember Red's high kick and the ball then zooming past me like a bullet. He may have pitched a ball or two just to put fright into me, but whatever his thoughts were, it worked. He fanned me. I should say he struck me out with my bat on my shoulder. His speed was just so great that I couldn't make up my mind to strike at any given throw.

We went down in order during the first three innings while they scored two runs. In the top of the fourth Jack Grantham connected with a fast ball that went between two outfielders for a double. All the while I had been playing errorless ball at first, but the truth is I didn't feel comfortable, due to my cleats. I had never worked out in cleats, much less played in them. The next two batters struck out and it looked like Grantham would die on second base as it was my turn to bat. I'm sure our coach would have put in another batter if he had had a pinch hitter in whom he had any confidence.

There was Jack on second and me at the plate, literally

scared to death of getting hit by one of Red's cannonballs. He
threw a strike and then a ball inside to scare me. Mr. Fenton,
our coach on the side lines, said for me to strike at the next one.
So I made up my mind to swing regardless of where the next
pitch might be. Sure, I saw him wind up. Sure, I saw his high
kick. And most surely I saw the ball start toward me. Then I
closed my eyes and swung out of sheer fright. The unbelievable
happened. I connected squarely with the ball as if I knew how, as
if I expected it to happen. All the time I knew it was a miracle.
Nobody knew my eyes were closed when I hit the ball except me.
The ball went over the first baseman's head. As I ran to first
Red stared in disbelief as if to say, "How could that spindly-
legged freshman hit my best fastball?" The ball rolled past the
right fielder and Mr. Fenton waved me on to second base with a
sweeping arm motion. I ran slightly outside the first base line
in order to make a good turn, and as I crossed the first base bag,
disaster struck. Remember, I said I hadn't worked out in cleats.
Well, as I crossed the base my cleats stuck in the bag just
enough to trip me. Then, there occurred the most embarrassing
fall I have ever had in my life. Running hard, I stumbled and fell
headlong into the dirt before sliding about ten feet further. Dirt
was in my uniform, under my belt, all over my face and in my
mouth, and my cap was askew. I jumped up and made it safely
back to first without being thrown out. Imagine how I felt. With
eyes closed I had hit a two bagger which turned out to be only a
single because of the baseball shoes, my first pair of cleats. But
guess what? I knocked in Jack Grantham for our only run of the
game which we lost by a score I can't remember at all. All I
remember are those new shoes and getting an eyes-closed hit off
Red Godbold. Oh yes, I also remember how proud my brother
was of me. You see, I never told him about my eyes being closed
when I swung.

When I was young, I doubt that they had even started
licensing automobile drivers. So, it was up to the family to
decide when a youth was old enough and mature enough to drive
a car. I practiced driving our T-Model Ford off the road on the
narrow dirt roads on our farm where it was impossible to hit
anything solid. If I lost control, all that happened was that I
would run into the cotton or corn planted up to the edge of the
road.

When I was fourteen, my father and older brother said I was
ready to drive on the open road.

The purpose of my first trip was to get some groceries in
town, and also the newspaper the postman did not bring that

day due to its being a holiday of some kind. Our holidays differed from those in most of the states as Mississippi had been a part of the Confederacy. We had a different Memorial Day than northern states and we had a holiday to honor Jefferson Davis, the President of the Confederacy, the only President the Confederacy ever had.

About a mile from home, while cruising along at about twenty-five miles an hour, I was really enjoying myself, when a mother hog and a brood of five-pound pigs, ran out of the weeds on the side of the road directly into my path. I could not stop or swerve in time, and a rear wheel hit one of the pigs. I could feel it hit, and stopped as soon as I could.

In the road about fifty yards back was a writhing, turning, twisting pig trying to get on his feet and follow the others who had gone into the weeds and road ditch. I picked up the poor little pig and hoped so badly I could get him to stand alone, but he couldn't. Each time I placed him on his feet his rear end gave way and settled to the ground. I could tell the poor little thing's back was broken.

It was so upsetting that I didn't want to continue to town on the errand. Instead, I put the little pig on the seat by me and patted him on the way home. But it was no use, the pig was fatally injured and died a few minutes after I got home with him. I was holding the little pig in my arms when he died.

The idea of killing a little helpless pig was too much for me to cope with. I broke into tears despite all the family members telling me it wasn't my fault. All their reasoning didn't do any good and I refused to drive the car again for almost a year.

We had dug a drainage ditch along the south border of our farm, which was along the back side of it. Across the ditch was a small farm that had never been cleared of trees and brush. Years before, a tornado had swept over it and blown down most of the large trees, and it had become a mass of dead trees, brush, vines, and wild shrubs to the point where it could hardly be penetrated by walking through it. We couldn't hunt there because the owner, a Mr. Wolfe, had put up NO TRESPASSING and NO HUNTING signs. It was obvious he wanted to be alone.

We kids seldom saw Mr. Wolfe. He had a very small house secluded from the small dirt road which his home faced. His house was about three hundred yards from the road and could not be seen from it. We thought Mr. Wolfe was sort of strange as he led such an isolated life and visited no one. He had no visible way of making a living; none of his land was in cultivation. Papa thought he was a moonshiner, but his house was so far from our land that Papa could never smell any mash fermenting or any whiskey being distilled.

Pigs entered into the picture to reveal what Mr. Wolfe did for a living. In the late fall when crops had been harvested, we let our pigs run free in the woods either on our farm or on other people's property. Our pigs didn't pay any attention to the NO TRESPASSING and NO HUNTING signs.

At the time we had a mother hog, or sow, with about six small pigs that followed her closely and rooted alongside her wherever she went. The sow and her pigs frequently roamed onto Mr. Wolfe's land, but we assumed they never went as far as Mr. Wolfe's house, about a quarter of a mile from our property line. Sometime in the afternoon or early evening, the sow usually came home from her foraging in the woods. The little pigs would be strung out in a line behind her.

One afternoon in late fall they didn't come home on time. Knowing they had gone in the direction of Mr. Wolfe's woods, we decided, right before dark, to go in search of them.

Just before reaching our property line we heard grunting and oinking sounds. We called to them, but there was no response except a continuation of the strange sounds. When we got to the ditch, which was free of water, we found them. The sow was trying to make it up the bank, but she would lose her footing and roll back to the bottom each time she attempted to climb out. The pigs were all around her. They could hardly stand alone, and when attempting to do so they would look like newly born pigs on their shaky legs. They were large enough to climb the bank themselves, but couldn't even get halfway up before losing their balance and rolling to the bottom. This was the funniest scene I had ever seen in my life and it soon became obvious they were drunk almost to the point of passing out. In fact, two of them seemed asleep on the bottom of the ditch, for they were making no effort to climb the bank.

Papa knew right off that they were drunk and he said, "These pigs have gotten into some of the fermented mash Mr. Wolfe has made and poured out on the ground. He must have made some that he couldn't distill. They are as drunk as hoot owls, we will have to haul them back home."

He sent Louis and me for the wagon. We ran as fast as we could to the barn, harnessed two mules and hitched them to the wagon. We then headed back to the scene at the ditch. Papa had kept watch while we were gone.

When we got back, he said, "Two more of them have gone to sleep."

He could just as well have said, "Two more of them have passed out."

The pigs weighed about ten pounds each so they were no problem to load into the wagon, but it took all three of us lifting and struggling to get the mother hog into the wagon. Then we had to hold her to keep her from jumping out.

On the way back to the pig-fenced area near the barn, Papa said, "Now I know Mr. Wolfe is a moonshiner, but without the pigs and their drunken state I could never be sure."

Suddenly, Papa said, "Darn, [almost like cursing to him] now I know who has been stealing our corn. It has been stolen a little at a time but quite a lot of it is missing. Mr. Wolfe has been using our corn to make his mash for whiskey distilling."

Papa had noticed ears of corn had been broken from a number of corn stalks near the place where our land joined Mr. Wolfe's. Part of the area had been planted to corn and part to cotton. It was one of the few years when we had a good corn crop as that part of the Delta was not really good corn country. The disappearing corn continued to the point where about one third of the ears had been taken from a large area, but not all had been taken from any certain spot. This was pretty good proof someone wanted to hide his thievery.

What happened next is something we didn't talk about outside the family for years and years, maybe never, as far as I can remember. It was because we were embarrassed to talk about it.

One bright night when the moon was full and when the corn was ripened enough to pull and store, Papa said he would be gone for a while and wanted to see if he could catch someone stealing corn. He knew the conditions were just right for a thief. As he left the house he picked up his old ten-gauge shotgun, the one I shot the hole in the roof with. We didn't like to see him take his gun with him but on the other hand we didn't know whether the corn thief was armed with a pistol or rifle, or not. So, no one, not even Mother, said a word.

We said nothing and hoped nothing would happen, but there was dead silence among us for almost an hour. We were all reading or studying and waiting for the moment Papa's leather boots would crunch on the back porch.

After about an hour and a half of waiting, the silence was suddenly broken by two gun blasts at very close intervals. We knew it sounded like a shotgun and feared the worst. Still, we were glad it didn't sound like a rifle or revolver, because it meant Papa was doing the shooting.

In about fifteen minutes Papa came in the back door. Of course, we couldn't wait to find out what happened.

He said he had made his way carefully into the corn field and had gotten a place near where we had hauled out the drunken pigs. There he decided to sit down on one of the corn rows and wait for awhile. It was cool and a slight breeze rustled the corn leaves around so they were quite noisy. After awhile he heard a tearing sound as if someone were tearing an ear of corn off the stalk.

"It was a distinct sound," he said, "and then I knew it was a person when I heard the sound a second time."

He then cautiously stood up and circled around to his left so that he could look down the rows of corn. The corn thief was moving slowly along the rows pulling an ear of corn from about one out of every four of the stalks. He was only about forty yards away.

"I knew he was going away and had his back toward me, but I also knew he was too close for what I had in mind. I just waited until he was about ten yards farther along the rows and then aimed near the ground and fired. He yelled at the top of his voice, threw the sack of corn down and ran. I pumped in another shell and fired low again," Papa said.

The man yelled, "Don't shoot, don't shoot," but kept running.

"I have the sack of corn on the back porch," he said.

Not a one of us ever repeated that story for many years, but the next week Papa had to go to Dr. Wasson for some minor treatment.

When being treated he asked, "Dr. Wasson, do you know our neighbor, [that was using the word carelessly] Mr. Wolfe?"

"Yes," was the reply, "in fact, he was in here yesterday. I picked a few shot out of his skin. One or two were infected, so he came to me. I wouldn't tell you this, Gilbert, except that he said he had an accident."

"Some accident," our father said he replied, "Maybe his wife shot him."

Can you imagine what it is like to have the banks in which you have your money deposited, money necessary for daily living, closed in such a way that you can't get any of your money out?

That's what happened in early 1933 to thousands of banks when the President ordered all banks closed until their books could be inspected and it could be determined whether they were either solvent or broke. The only two banks in which my father had money were closed in this way. We were not able to get any of our money out at all for approximately ninety days and then only a small part of it. We had no money and no way to get any. This meant we had no way to buy food for our family or the tenant farmers on our farm. We almost became desperate wondering when the banks would re-open or if they ever would. There was no government guarantee of deposits in those day.

All of us had plenty to eat, but our meals weren't balanced. We had corn meal ground from corn we produced, salt pork, milk, butter, and some vegetables as it was springtime. We had almost no flour. During those days, we had biscuits for breakfast with butter and molasses. We ate cornbread at all other meals. I'm sure the Negro tenant farmers on our farm had even less.

But happily, we had a good corn crop the year before and our corn crib was bulging with ears of corn. Papa heard that Mr. Hammarstein, a Jewish farmer and merchant, needed some corn for two of his riding horses. What was unusual about Mr. Hammarstein was that he was both a Jew and a farmer. None of the Jewish people we knew were farmers; they were merchants of one kind or another. Mr. Hammarstein was the exception.

So Papa saw Mr. Hammarstein one day on the street and asked him if he wanted to buy some top quality corn. Good quality corn was a rarity in the Delta because it is not good corn country.

Mr. Hammarstein said, " Yes, I need a hundred bushels of corn for my horses, but it must be delivered to my barn."

In the following conversation they got together on terms and delivery. They then shook hands over the deal. We were to deliver the hundred bushels of corn for 25 cents per bushel. Papa knew that was about 10 cents a bushel less than the corn was worth, but he felt that he had no choice. Mr. Hammarstein had the cash—that was the most important point in the deal.

When loading our wagon with corn we almost drooled over the idea that our family would have 25 dollars cash with which to buy those things which were most necessary for the family.

At supper that night all were in a good mood and thinking about what Papa could do with the money when he said, "Now, I want to tell everybody we promised to pay the church $15 this year and we haven't paid them anything so far. I think it is only fair that we give $5 of the $25 to the church."

For a minute we were all shocked. We were thinking, "We need that money so badly and he is going to give the church $5 of it." We could hardly believe what we were hearing, but that's the way it was.

During those years, Papa wasn't even going to church, but I

guess because his father had been a minister-farmer, he knew churches had their problems, too. In a way, we were all proud that Papa had kept his word to the church.

I often thought the term, "His word is as good as his bond" was invented to apply to my father in the first place.

We had prospered, like those people who played the stock market, in 1928 and 1929 and even a little later. By this time I was driving and had things pretty much to myself as Hubert had already left home and was living in Jackson. This meant I had no brother with whom to compete for the car. I had great plans for taking girls riding in it.

Papa decided to go all out and bought a Buick sedan. It was something to see and we were so proud of it. He had not seen his brother who lived in Palestine, Texas, for about twenty-five years, and decided we would go to see him, with me driving. What a trip! About 350 miles with paved roads all the way from Monroe, Louisiana to Shreveport, Louisiana. Between those two cities, it was 96 miles.

When we got out of Monroe, Papa said, "Let's make it in two and a half hours, an average speed of almost forty miles an hour."

Boy, that seemed pretty fast to me, but by holding the speed near fifty miles an hour we did get to Shreveport in two and a half hours and we bragged about that for several years. We made it to Palestine and while there we drove into town from my uncle's farm and parked in front of a house on a gravel street.

I elected to stay in the car while my father and uncle went inside. After they had been gone a few minutes, it seemed I could smell something burning and then, I saw smoke rising on each side of the vented hood. Hoods lifted on each side in those days. As quickly as possible I jumped out and raised the hood on the left side. Lo, and behold! A small flame was burning some oil near the starter. There was no fire extinguisher and no water nearby so I did the only thing I could think of. As fast as I could move, I reached down and got cupped hands full of gravel and sand from the street and threw it on the flame. At first, it looked as if I would lose the battle, but then I began to gain and the flame started receding. In a very short while I had it out. How can anyone be so thankful, I wondered?

Not long after we returned home the newspapers began writing about the depression we were in. About that time, the stock market was very low and lots of banks were going broke. What upset us most, though, was that the price of cotton sagged to new lows. Everything pointed to very hard times ahead.

164

When Papa bought the Buick, he made a substantial down payment on it and was to make monthly payments to a company in Greenwood until it was paid for. As our prospects for making money off our cotton sagged, Papa could see that he couldn't meet all of his obligations.

He had made a payment on the car on the first of the month, but on the 5th he announced at supper, "I might as well tell you folks that we can't afford to keep that car, so I locked the garage doors a few minutes ago. I don't want anybody driving it again. Tomorrow, Wilson, I want you to walk to town and get Aunt Inez to call the agency in Greenwood and tell them to come get the car."

To say the very least, I was shocked; just stunned speechless for a moment.

In a minute or two I said, "Papa, you just made a payment on it the other day. We can keep it for the rest of the month."

All the time I could see my hopes and dreams of driving that car and impressing the girls with it evaporating into thin air.

He said, "No, we won't keep it any longer. First, because we know we will be giving it up, and second, because you will just become more miserable about losing it as next month nears."

That's the way it was. We gave the car up and didn't have another one as long as I remained home until I went away to college.

At the time, I thought Papa was cruel regarding the car, but as time passed, I began to respect the way he handled the matter. As it turned out, the deepest, darkest days of the famous depression were still ahead.

Chapter 17

PAPA AND THE MADAM

The only time I ever saw my father naked was when the boat drifted away from shore when we were camping by the lake. He stripped off all his clothes and waded out as far as he could in the lake with a very light block of wood to throw to me in case I faltered in trying to swim to the boat. He did this when he couldn't swim a lick. Papa was a good physical specimen. He was about 55 at the time and weighed 175. He was exactly six feet tall and had boundless energy.

But what was he really like? We never said grace at meals until after he had returned from his father's funeral in Alabama in 1928. After that we always had grace at every meal, except breakfast when we could never sit down together. Why did he change so suddenly? What happened in Alabama that caused him to want to say thanks to God? I wish I had asked him, but I waited too late.

One of his blessings was recited a thousand or more times: "Kind Father, look upon us with mercy, forgive us our sins, bless this food to its intended purpose, we ask in the Name of Jesus Christ, Amen."

The other, and it was always one or the other: " We thank Thee, Heavenly Father, for all the blessings of life. Forgive us our sins, we ask in the Name of Thy Son, Jesus Christ, Amen."

Papa almost never showed affection. I saw him kiss my mother only half a dozen times, once being when he returned from a trip to Texas and another after his father's death. But I did often see him enter the back door of the kitchen, near where Mother was working at the stove. Quite often he would pinch her backside and he could always expect her reaction to be, "Gilbert, quit that, act your age." That would be the end of it. Papa always referred to Mother as, "The Madam."

Papa didn't show affection to his kids. Of course, the girls always kissed him upon their return home for visits. We boys shook hands with him at the time. Oh, but I fooled him one time when he was about 75 or 80. Upon returning home from my own home in Kansas, I was so pleased to see him that I brushed aside his extended hand and gave him a bear hug. When he returned the hug with pressure of his own, I resolved never to fail to hug him when I visited. I lived up to that until he died in his sleep at ninety-two. Two of my brothers were standing by when I hugged him and I know they hadn't seen him hugged by one of the boys before.

What kind of man is it who will give 5 dollars to the church when he has a family and only 25 dollars to his name?

What kind of man is it who will charge his tenant farmers, Negroes, six percent interest on money or food he advances them, while paying the bank more than that?

Is it often you see a man who will ask that his car be immediately repossessed when he has it paid up for 25 days in the future?

Papa had a temper, but I never saw him mistreat a kid or a mule when he was angry. He was always cool and self-possessed when he punished us. He had dark moods which Mother called the "blues" that lasted for a day or two, at times. We always knew how he cured them. He took an ax and sledgehammer to the woods and worked to his physical limits for several hours. When he returned with his clothes completely saturated with his own sweat, physically exhausted, we knew he had conquered the "blues" and his mood would be bright and sunny.

Papa couldn't understand why none of his six boys ever gave any indication of wanting to be a farmer. Thank goodness, he never asked us why.

We would each have said, "It's too much like being a slave to your work, and there is no future in it."

That's the way we saw it because our farm experiences were in the days before mechanized farming came about. Now, everything is done with machinery. Our farm work was physical drudgery for twelve or more hours a day.

When my mother was rearing her family of nine kids in the late teens and the twenties, women of that era would have said, "Isn't it nice that we mothers don't have to put up with the things mothers of 1850 had to make do with?"

My mother would probably have agreed with that. She would have just automatically thought she was better off and had less problems to face.

When I ask myself that, I can't find a thing different of any importance that would have made my mother's life any easier.

My mother darned socks with needle and thread; she had to peddle the power for her sewing machine; she cooked on a wood stove (but it did have a temperature indicator on the oven door); she ironed with a heavy cast iron flatiron heated either on the fire in the fireplace or the stove; she read by kerosene lamp light, she walked or rode a wagon almost everywhere before we got a car in 1925; she bore her children at home (twelve of them); she worked the entire day except for a short rest period at noon; she pumped water by hand pump; she washed our clothes in a tub with a corrugated washboard; and she used an outdoor privy just as the entire family did. I don't think the mother of 1850 had it any worse.

Of course, as we kids got old enough by stair-steps in ages, we helped out and all quickly knew what we were to do. But Mother's work kept her busy from before daylight until after dark. I wish I had asked her if she thought her lot an unfair or unjust one, or if she thought her life was too demanding in the way of drudgery, but I didn't. That seems to have been the story with all of us kids. I don't think any of us asked about the things that really mattered of our parents until too late.

Mother seemed so easy going, almost stoical, to me at times. She didn't seem to have those "highs" and "lows" most people have. She seemed to bend with the wind rather than break. It seemed to me that she had few decisions to make; they were made for her by someone else or by circumstances she couldn't have changed, anyway. But I found out when I was eleven that she could really put her foot down and stonewall it when she thought she had to.

It was in 1925 that Papa had an invitation to ride with a relative who was going down to the Rio Grande Valley, near Harlingen, Texas, to see the relative's father, who was a truck gardener. Although the trip was long and arduous, Papa came back feeling like an enthusiastic kid over a new toy.

He was completely sold on truck gardening down there. Also, the orange and grapefruit trees impressed him. With all of us boys to help, he could see our family getting rich farming in the Valley. The old Daniel Boone spirit was really showing and he came back with immediate plans to sell our farm and move to the Harlingen area.

Such a move at the time would have taken Mother away from her mother, Grandma White, and her two sisters who lived nearby. To be 1,000 miles from them with few prospects of getting back for a visit was just too much for her to take.

What conversation took place between Mother and Papa and among other family members, I can't vouch for, but Hubert gave me his version.

He said, "When Papa told Mother his plans, she told him she would think it over but didn't really like the idea. The next morning she told him that she wouldn't move to the Rio Grande Valley under any circumstances. If he were determined to go, he would just have to go without her."

I never did know any more than that except that the atmosphere around the house was cool and tense for quite a long time.

Ultimately, Papa got over his disappointment, but Mother had prevailed in that crisis. So, I know she had a mind of her own and wasn't afraid to assert herself if she thought her actions were for the family welfare.

Mother's true colors also came through years later when I was a senior in college, home for the Thanksgiving holidays.

I had been moping around all morning and at intervals would lean on the mantle over the fireplace and stare into the fire in the fireplace.

Mother noticed that and after a while asked, "Wilson, you aren't acting like you usually do. Why are you staring into that fire like that? Aren't you happy to be home for Thanksgiving?"

My answer came only when I was certain no one else was listening. "Mother, I guess I ought to tell you first that I have met the girl that I think I want to marry. I haven't even told her I love her but I know she is the one. We have been dating about two months and I'm sure, but I don't know if she is. She's from Kansas and it is too far away for her to go home for the holiday. She and two other students are in the dormitory. I guess that's why I can't get into the Thanksgiving mood."

"Will they have Thanksgiving dinner?" Mother asked.

"No," I replied, "they will eat whatever the two Negro cooks fix for them in the dining hall."

"Well, I just can't enjoy Thanksgiving dinner for thinking about those girls being alone and without something special for Thanksgiving," Mother said. "Isn't there some way we could get your girl over here?" Mother continued.

"No, we have no car and neither does she, so there is nothing we can do," I lamented.

"Well, there is," Mother said with enthusiasm, "I'll just dress two chickens. You can hitchhike with them to Cleveland, and then arrange to have them cooked. Surely, the two cooks will do that since you are a bus boy in the dining hall."

What a great idea!

"Who but you, Mother, could have come up with such a plan?" I asked.

She fixed the chickens and shortly after noon I caught a ride to Cleveland which was only forty-five miles away. By mid-afternoon I had taken the chickens to the dining hall where the two cooks gladly agreed to prepare them for the belated Thanksgiving dinner for the four of us.

Then after a short search, I found Grace playing cards with the other girls in her dormitory lobby. When I told them of the plans for a Thanksgiving feast they were elated. Now, we could celebrate.

It was that night that I told Grace I was in love with her. Within six weeks we were engaged and on August 18, 1989, we celebrated our fiftieth wedding anniversary.

Who knows? It may have been my dear mother who waved her magic wand and helped us determine our future.